The Blue Poppy and the Mustard Seed

A Mother's Story of Loss and Hope

The Blue Poppy and the Mustard Seed

A Mother's Story of Loss and Hope

By

KATHLEEN WILLIS MORTON

WISDOM PUBLICATIONS • BOSTON

Wisdom Publications
199 Elm Street
Somerville MA 02144 USA
www.wisdompubs.org

Library of Congress Cataloging-in-Publication Data
Willis Morton, Kathleen.
 The blue poppy and the musard seed : a mother's story of loss and hope / by Kathleen Willis Morton.
   p. cm.
 ISBN 0-86171-565-9 (pbk. : alk. paper)
1. Willis Morton, Kathleen. 2. Spiritual biography. 3. Grief—Religious aspects—Buddhism. 4. Buddhism. 5. InfantsDeath. I. Title.
 BQ996.I45 A3 2008
 294.3'4442092—dc22
 [B]
                          2008023221

12 11 10 09 08
5 4 3 2 1

Cover design by Pema Studios. Interior design by Dede Cummings. Set in Caslon 11.5/15.5. Cover and interior photograph © Lynne Jaeger Weinstein

"A Ritual to Read to Each Other" © 1960, 1998 by the Estate of William Stafford. Reprinted from *The Way It Is: New & Selected Poems* with the permission of Graywolf Press, Saint Paul, Minnesota.

Wisdom Publications' books are printed on acid-free paper and meet the guidelines for permanence and durability of the Production Guidelines for Book Longevity of the Council on Library Resources.

Printed in the United States of America.

This book was produced with environmental mindfulness. We have elected to print this title on 30% PCW recycled paper. As a result, we have saved the following resources: 27 trees, 19 million BTUs of energy, 2,369 lbs. of greenhouse gases, 9,832 gallons of water, and 1,263 lbs. of solid waste. For more information, please visit our website, www.wisdompubs.org. This paper is also FSC certified. For more information, please visit www.fscus.org.

A Ritual To Read To Each Other

If you don't know the kind of person I am
and I don't know the kind of person you are
a pattern that others made may prevail in the world
and following the wrong god home we may miss our star.

For there is many a small betrayal in the mind,
a shrug that lets the fragile sequence break
sending with shouts the horrible errors of childhood
storming out to play through the broken dyke.

And as elephants parade holding each elephant's tail,
but if one wanders the circus won't find the park,
I call it cruel and maybe the root of all cruelty
to know what occurs but not recognize the fact.

And so I appeal to a voice, to something shadowy,
a remote important region in all who talk:
though we could fool each other, we should consider—
lest the parade of our mutual life get lost in the dark.

For it is important that awake people be awake,
or a breaking line may discourage them back to sleep;
the signals we give—yes or no, or maybe—
should be clear: the darkness around us is deep.

—William Stafford

The Blue Poppy and the Mustard Seed

A Mother's Story of Loss and Hope

Still Moment of Mystery

There is only one truth, one law, in all the world
and the six realms of existence, too:
all things are impermanent.
—*The Buddha, to Kisa Gotami*

I WAS CHANGING MY SON LIAM'S DIAPER when I noticed his left hand and part of his arm had started to turn dusky-plum blue.

"Liam," tears came again, "you have to let go now, baby." My knees sank to the floor. I folded over the bed where he was lying and pulled him to my side. He was so thin it hurt me to hold him.

"Liam, if you need to go, you should go." I had been repeating that phrase for forty-five days when I could gather the strength. Every day, I knew it might be his last. I gave him permission to die. Hospice workers and Tibetan Buddhist tradition say to do that so the person can have a peaceful death. I was desperate to give back something to Liam even if it was only a peaceful death. Every night as I held Liam bundled up between his father and me in bed I thought, *Please not tonight. Just let him live until the morning.*

Every morning I didn't move until I knew that he was still breathing. Then I'd kiss him, and I'd think, *not today. I hope he doesn't die today.*

When I saw his hand was blue I knew it wouldn't be long.

"You can't hold on any longer, Liam. It's time for you to let go."

My father-in-law, who is a heart surgeon, had told Chris, my husband, and me that Liam's limbs might discolor eventually because his heart didn't circulate enough blood.

My voice was soft and shaky like a butterfly flying against the wind when I finally got Chris on the phone at work.

"Chris, you have to come home. His hand is blue. You have to come home."

"I'll be right there."

Chris had only been at work for a few hours, and it was only his second day back. He didn't want to go back to work, but we had no idea how long Liam would live—and we had to reach for some normalcy, now almost seven weeks after his birth. When we left the Neonatal Intensive Care Unit at Emmanuel Legacy Hospital, Liam's cardiologist had said, "If he's still here in a week, call me. I'll want to see him again."

When Liam had been home a week we decided not to call the doctors anymore.

"Will they be able to tell you anything that will make a difference in his condition?" my father-in-law had asked.

"No," we'd answered, remembering the grim diagnosis that was documented in his medical records:

```
The child has sustained extensive bilateral cerebral
hypoxia. This seems to be a more global change that
would suggest more of a global perfusion problem,
rather than emboli . . . The prognosis, which is very
limited for this child, has been discussed with his fam-
ily. His prognosis is of such severity, I think the fam-
```

ily should be apprised of this in order to make decision on his care.
     I would support their decision either way, to avoid
futile care (in view of his very serious neurological
findings) . . .

Futile care. That was the phrase that hit me the hardest. How could it make sense that medical care for any child would be futile?

I FINISHED changing Liam's diaper and swaddled him in a blanket. I put a hat on his head even though it was June 27. He should have been fat and warm, bouncing and giggling on my knee. Instead, I took his temperature every couple of hours to make sure it had not slipped below ninety-two degrees. If it were really low, Chris would unbutton his shirt and undress Liam to his diapers. Then they would lay, bare chest to bare chest, under the comforter, with the light streaming in the bedroom window, until Liam was warm again.

Liam's eyes were dulled and glassy. He was somewhere trapped inside a body that, at the time of his birth, had looked perfect in every way on the outside. His skin was downy like a white peach. He had our coloring. His hair was amber, a subtle blending of his father's auburn-brown and my strawberry blonde. When he was born a plump 7 lbs. 8 oz. he resembled me. Then his cherub frame waned to probably less than 4 lbs. I had books on my shelf that were heavier than he was in the end, when he took on the sharp angles of his father's face. Inside—his heart and his mind, his wisdom and his skill—he had reached his fullest potential at almost seven weeks old.

"He won't walk. He won't talk. He won't be able to feed himself. You will be lucky if he recognizes you as his parents," Liam's neurologist had said at our initial meeting. With each sentence he spoke, the tide of my blood pulled back. I felt my face blanch, and my jaw and body slacken. "He might not even be aware of his surroundings. And I'm not sure he'll even be able to think. Let me make this really clear. I'm not talking about mild damage. I'm not talking about medium damage. This is severe." His eyes were unwavering.

CHRIS ARRIVED HOME. But that was all we could do—just be with him. I didn't want to put Liam down. I sat in the white chair by the bookshelf and held him. I picked up a thin copy of *The Life of the Buddha* by Venerable Dr. Hammalawa Saddhatissa, and I began reading it out loud to Liam. I sat, and read, and held my son all day because I couldn't bear to let him go. I didn't know anything else to do. I didn't want to do anything else. I didn't get up to eat or pee. I sat and held my son all day. Chris was across the room sitting on the couch for most of the day too. I didn't fully notice what he was doing. I just felt the barely-there weight of my son in my arms as I read to him about an ordinary person who had found a way, a path, out of suffering.

That night, I lay next to Liam on the bed. I turned on the TV that was at the end of the bed. I didn't really want to watch TV. I just didn't want to watch my son die. The square room felt like a TV screen. I watched from outside myself. I saw Liam on the bed wrapped in his blankets: motionless, silent, still breathing. I sat next to him, propped up on the pillows, and stared at the happy everything-will-be-okay-in-a-half-hour world on TV. I was still on the surface like a calm ocean, but underneath I was dark and shifting restlessly. I felt I should be talking to Liam. I felt I should be doing something. I felt I should hold him and comfort him. I flicked off the TV and turned to him. Each breath could be his last. I didn't want to miss it, but it was too hard to focus my attention on him. I tried to talk to him.

"Liam, Mommy's here. Don't be afraid." Hysteria rose to the surface of my voice like a shark with obsidian eyes. I gasped and choked on my words. I couldn't talk to him and stay calm at the same time. I didn't want to disturb his dying. I didn't want to distract him with my moans and cries that might hold him to this imperfect body and world. I turned the TV back on and watched every crisis resolve on the half-hour. I floated above my grief. Chris was upstairs meditating. My son lay dying beside me. Though I couldn't look at him, I felt the rise and fall of his breath throughout that Thursday evening, and into the night when all three of us curled up under the covers and let the dark of the room enclose us.

That night I didn't make my panicked plea for one more night. I just pulled Liam close and whispered with my lips touching his soft cool temple. "Mommy has you, Mommy has you." I wasn't sure he could hear me, but I hoped that he could feel my words.

The moment of Liam's death came gently near dawn as he lay on the bed between his father and me.

I heard a little whine just as I was beginning to doze off. I was instantly wide-awake. "Chris, turn on the light." I looked at the clock; it was 1:58 AM. Liam whined again softly. He took a breath, and then did not. I moved the blankets away from his body so I could see it. Chris and I were vigilant for I don't know how long. Liam was lying on his right side with his right arm bent and his palm beneath his head. His left arm was folded across his chest with his other palm down on the bed. By chance it was the same position the Buddha was in when he passed into *parinirvana*. Chris and I were propped up on our forearms lying on our stomachs beside him. Liam's belly and chest did not rise again. We were still. The world was still. It was the moment we knew would come. That mysterious moment that connects this life with the next. The only moment that all of us can be sure will eventually come someday.

We rose slowly and sat on either side of the bed. Every bit of warmth left his body as I sat reciting, as best I could, the Tibetan Buddhist prayers prescribed for the moment of death. I closed my eyes. I heard my cries as if from a distance. I forced myself not to cry so that Liam could pass away undisturbed. We didn't touch him. I didn't want to hold Liam back.

In that mysterious moment, this is what I remember seeing in my mind: There was amber light. There was warmth. There was a person with long hair and a beige dress with her back to me who squatted down, opened her arms, and scooped up a plump, pink, laughing baby who kicked and waved his arms. I thought the baby must be Liam though I didn't completely recognize him in a healthy body. The woman walked away , carrying the baby who was looking over her shoulder. I felt calm. I noticed I had stopped choking on my dammed-up tears and gasping for breath. As I slowly opened my eyes I heard a small voice say, "Mommy." With my eyes then fully open, a thought popped into my head. It was Liam, and he knew I would want to hear him speak just once. It hadn't occurred to me until just then that I would never hear my son call me *Mommy*. And yes, I would have wanted to hear it. Those were things—speaking, laughing, thriving—that he would never do, no matter how long he lived.

I turned to Chris and looked over his shoulder to the clock. It was 5:30 AM. Three and a half hours had passed into nothing.

"We should clean him up before he gets too stiff," I said. "Will you do it? I can't."

Chris had to do a lot of things I was not strong enough to do.

PRETENDING EVERYTHING WAS OKAY was something I could do, had to do sometimes, and was something I got good at faking for short amounts of time.

When Liam was four weeks old we had to buy him preemie clothes because all his newborn clothes, hand-me-downs from my sisters-in-law and crisp new outfits from his baby shower, were all too big. We went to the same store where we had ordered Liam's blue-and-white gingham stroller with a chrome chassis and white-wall tires. The saleswoman recognized us. We had spent a long time with her while placing our order for the stroller and had spoken to her several times on the phone. As we looked through the small selection of clothes for premature babies she was silent. She didn't congratulate us. She didn't come over to dote on Liam. I could feel her sad eyes on us. She looked away when I looked up to meet her gaze. I tried to pick the cutest onesie from the sad assortment on the rack for my son who was not born prematurely—just dying that way.

Chris and I loved to push Liam in his buggy up and down Hawthorne Street by our home and pretend we were a normal family.

"Oh, he's perfect," the man at the Ben & Jerry's shop said. He put his arm around the pregnant woman standing next to him and gave her a gentle squeeze. What we couldn't see behind my perfect son's soft, dark eyes was the tremendous global brain damage that robbed my son of the most basic of human survival instincts: to nurse, to cry, and to respond to the world around him.

"Yes," I said to the man. "He's perfect."

We encountered another couple on the street. "Oh, a redhead. We have a redhead too," said a woman holding their two-year-old. "Just wait till he's this age," the man gushed to us. "They're such a blast."

"We can't wait," we beamed back.

Some people did notice that there was something a little different about Liam. "What a cutie," the owner of the bar on the corner said screwing up her nose. "He's got some snot on his cheek, though."

"No, that's his feeding tube. He's very sick."

"Oh." She didn't skip a beat. "Isn't it amazing what they can do with science these days?"

"Yeah," we both said. We just smiled. We didn't tell her that it was more amazing that science could do nothing for us, or for Liam.

"So, have you adjusted to the shock of being new parents yet?" she asked.

Chris and I stared at each other looking for an answer.

"I guess that means no," she said.

We were in shock but not because we were "new" parents. Parenting a terminally ill newborn, assessing all the information the doctors delivered to us, and deciding what was best for Liam, we felt like we had done a lifetime of parenting in just a week. We had never had time to feel new.

CHRIS DID, however, take care of Liam with the adoring attention that any new father would, till the very end.

Chris went into the bathroom and ran hot water over a washcloth to clean Liam for the last time. He returned and pulled Liam, who was still lying on the bed, a little nearer to him so he could change his diaper. Chris turned Liam on his back. I winced and turned my head away. The right side of Liam's face and the corner of his right eye were dark cherry-red with still blood that had begun to pool on the side of his body on which he was lying. His eyes were basalt, skin like lilies-of-the-valley, lips the color of gray-blue flannel.

As I stood up I saw Chris cleaning Liam's bottom, wiping away the tar-like excrement released when his energy let go of his body. Chris held Liam's cold feet and wiped him clean with slow, deliberate strokes, taking care to make sure he wiped away all the dirt, just like he did every day in the same gentle manner. He did not grimace. If he was too overwhelmed, like I was, to touch his son's cold, dead body he didn't show it.

"I'm sorry you have to do that, honey," I said, "I just can't."

"It's okay. He's my baby. I love him, and I want to clean him." His voice was a thin trickle.

"I'll call Sharon," I said leaving them alone in the room. Sharon was Liam's hospice nurse who came over every other day. She didn't sound as if I'd woken her when she answered the phone, though it was dawn.

"Sharon, it's Katie." My voice was flat.

She said, slowly raising her voice to make the one word into a question, "Hi?"

"Liam passed."

Sharon exhaled. "Okay. Do you want me to come over now or do you want some time alone with Liam?" She knew some people were afraid to be alone with their dead children. We had talked about what would happen when the time came. She had to come over to officially pronounce Liam dead.

"No, you don't have to come now. He actually passed away at 1:58, but we didn't want to call you then."

"Okay, I'll come over in a couple of hours. Did you call the funeral home?"

"Not yet."

"Do you need me to call for you?"

"No."

"Okay, I'll see you in a couple of hours."

Chris called the funeral home. The man who answered told Chris that they wouldn't be open till 9 AM.

We were grateful to have a few extra hours with Liam. We lay on the bed with Liam between us.

"Maybe we should read him *Horton Hears a Who!* one last time," I suggested.

Chris's voice undulated with tears held back as he read. It was the story we read to Liam every day when he was hooked up to all the monitors and IVs for the first week of his life that he spent in the NICU, the Neonatal Intensive Care Unit. Chris dissolved into tears half way through the story when he read, "I'll just have to save him. Because, after all, a person's a person, no matter how small."

We reached over Liam to each other, and cried, and waited.

A Mourning Walk
Around the World

We travel, initially, to lose ourselves; and we travel, next, to
find ourselves . . . I travel in large part in search of
hardship—both my own, which I want to feel, and others',
which I need to see. Travel in that sense guides us toward a
better balance of wisdom and compassion.
—*Pico Iyer*

C HRIS QUIT HIS JOB AS A BREWER. I quit my job at the
bookstore. We booked a trip around the world. I told everyone we were running away and tried to sound sarcastic, or
matter-of-fact, or something that didn't belie the blackness I felt. I
wanted to walk away forever going nowhere, and lie down and die at
the same time.

Everyone we told said, "How awesome. I wish I could go on that
trip." I wished they were going instead of me too. The trip didn't
seem as much like the privilege everyone thought it was, but rather
a consolation prize, a gift given to the ones who have lost. We were

setting off to wander, to remember together, gather sense, make account of the days we lived—as well as we could—with Liam waiting for the moment we'd have to let him go ahead, and to wonder together what life we would live next, having now let go of the future we planned. We could not predict what that life would be. We couldn't see it from where we stood in such a cold, dark place. We had, I felt, to walk there.

It would be a journey further than I knew I could go.

With the awkward steps of a diver beginning a shore dive, looking backward at the shifting sands and struggling to find sure footing, we left Portland, Oregon, on October 18, 1998.

THE NIGHT AIR was moist and sweet with plumeria blossoms when Chris and I made our way from the Kauai airport terminal to the Hertz office across the street. We rented a car and planned to save money by camping on the beaches. My throat was raw and painful. I was exhausted by the time we found our car in the lot of identical brown Chryslers. I lacked even the strength to muster much excitement about being in Hawaii, a place I had always wanted to go.

Hawaii was the first stop on our trip. We would travel from the West Coast of the United States all the way around the globe. With any luck, we would find ourselves on the other side of the enormous sea of grief surrounding us.

After we threw our packs in the trunk, I ran to the front of the car, out of sight, and threw up in the bushes. I pressed my forearm across my abdomen in a reflex motion to stabilize my C-section scar that was still raw, and new, and now aching from the violent spasms that purged half-digested airplane food and grief. I remembered thinking after we were told about Liam's prognosis that I would have my scar longer than I would have my son in my life.

We made our way to the Kauai youth hostel. Since it was late, we would spend the night there rather than trying to make camp in the dark. We were not really in the mood to make a lot of chitchat with the other guests, which we would have usually enjoyed. I felt like I just needed some peace and quiet, so we agreed to splurge a bit and get a private room where we could be together rather than in bunks in two different single-sex dorms.

I switched on the light once we got into the room. The cockroaches were so bold they didn't even bother to scatter, though there was nothing in the room to give them cover except for the sagging bed with sheets and blankets so dingy and limp they seemed to sigh. The rank smell of the room suited my mood. I slid the window open in its aluminum frame and dropped my body, still bloated from pregnancy weight, onto the bed. I let out a guttural moan and began to cry. Chris stood in the doorway as my grief swelled over him.

"What's wrong?" he asked. His shoulders dropped.

"What do you think is wrong? My son is dead. My throat hurts. I'm tired, and sick, and this place is disgusting."

"But you said you wanted to go on this trip," he said, dropping his pack to the floor, letting it hit the ground hard.

"I didn't say I wanted to go on this trip. I just didn't want to stay home. And I don't want to be here. I don't want to be anywhere. I just want Liam." My loud voice made Chris cringe. He quietly crossed the room, sat on the bed, slowly took a book out of his pack, and headed for the door again. At the doorway he stopped. He took a deep breath and reached out to me with his eyes, hazel like a sea darkened by an impending storm. But he turned and left me alone in the bare, dark room.

When Liam was alive, and slowly dying, our perspective was different. We didn't argue at all; time was too precious to spend any of it fighting. Since Liam passed, there was a tension between Chris and me that was growing. The tension was like a towline on a boat moored on a pitching sea. We strained against each other's hold, but it was that tension that held us together too. Without it, we both would have gone under in the force of the storm. We pulled and pushed against each other because it was the only way to stay upright at all. We were angry at life and at death, so we ended up being angry at each other.

When Chris came back into the hostel room I stirred from a half-sleep. I felt my eyes relax behind their lids when he turned off the light and came to bed. It was hard to be with him because there wasn't much room in my world that wasn't consumed with a deep sadness, but it was harder to be alone. He got under the covers. I whispered that I was sorry. He pulled me to him urgently; we kissed gently and his touch anchored me. The distant sound of the waves from the nearby Pacific calmed me. I dreamed of swimming in the ocean.

MOST OF THE TEN DAYS we spent in Kauai we spent on the beaches doing nothing, and it was exactly what I wanted to do. We hiked the Awaawapuhi Trail in the Waimea Canyon State Park.

We camped on Anini Beach for the first night. It was a lovely park on a white-sand cove. The waves were gentle. A young family had set up camp there too. From the looks of their site with its makeshift kitchen and palm-thatched living space it seemed like they planned to be there a while. The young mother often sat at the edge of the sea, with the warm water lapping at her toes, while her infant suckled, I imagined, wetly, with urgency at her breast. Often, holding Liam in my arms, I had felt time biting urgently at my heart. His life had been full with meaning, even though it was as short as a Hawaiian sunset.

I was soon overcome with an aching sickness, which had started brewing when we first landed. My sore throat turned into a flu that made sleeping on the thin inflatable mattress unbearable. Despite the beautiful view from our tent, I had to get away. We spent two nights at the Mohala Ke Ola Bed and Breakfast. I recouped quickly, and we returned to our tent and a different site, Salt Pond Beach, for the rest of our stay.

We hired an instructor to teach us how to scuba dive and spent a day in the Outrigger hotel's pool before going out for two days into the open waters. Chris and I had just passed the written test required as part of the scuba certification process and finished practicing in the pool when we drove out of the hotel driveway and passed a woman walking toward the hotel.

"Chris!" I startled him, as much as I myself was startled to see what I thought might be a hallucination, "I think that was our midwife. Back up."

As he steered the car in reverse I craned my neck to see if I was right. Had I just seen the registered nurse and certified midwife whom I had seen for my prenatal care? She was present at Liam's birth and assisted in his emergency surgical delivery.

The last time I saw her, she was holding Liam in her arms in her office, where we'd gone just to visit her, a week before he died. In her office was a print of what I remember to be a baby curled like a pearl in a shell. Yes, I had thought, looking at Liam curled in her arms saying unspoken good-byes. Yes, a jewel.

I couldn't believe she was standing in front of me on that very small island in the middle of the ocean, just after Chris and I had passed our test and were about to set out into the deep waters that lay all around us.

She seemed equally shocked to see us as we pulled alongside her and I called to her through the window. I didn't know what our unlikely meeting could have meant for her given the surprise and unfortunate outcome of Liam's birth; for me it felt like a sign that Liam would always be held in the space between me and anyone I would encounter. We all exchanged greetings and wished each other the best before we set out in different directions. Chris and I were headed to explore a depth we had never known.

UNDERWATER we had to learn new ways to communicate. There were only a few vital hand signals, which the instructor taught us: going up, going down, I'm okay, help, danger, out of air, go that way, hold hands, get with your buddy, you lead and I'll follow, slow down. It was a simple language. Minimal. Only the important things needed to be communicated. Grief was a lot like being under the ocean. Things didn't sound the same. The world moved more slowly. Simple objects were magnified; they signified something more than themselves. They seemed to communicate that there was another way to look at the world. Colors were intensified, or changed altogether, but so was the darkness. If I weren't careful the pressure around me would crush me.

Underwater we had to be aware of our breath and the fact that it might run out. Under the pressure of my son's absence I thought often about breath—his first, his last, and my own which was often stifled by sadness that was invisible and weighted like the atmosphere and the pressure of the ocean around us; our lives were running out like the air in our tanks.

The first time we went under and "blew bubbles," it was in a spot by an abandoned pier called Ahukini. A man coming out of the water said he saw a tiger shark. Our instructor shrugged him off and told us not to worry.

"You never have to outswim a shark," he said. "You just have to outswim the slowest swimmer."

We laughed more out of courtesy than genuine cheer as we geared up.

"Seriously," he said. "That guy is a chicken. Sharks are afraid of divers because of all the bubbles and gear. If one does come at you, just hit it; they want an easy meal, not one that puts up a fight." I wondered if I would be strong enough to fight off anything. Had the Buddha's teachings geared me up for what I needed to swim through? I was laughing, but inside I was fighting back a shifting fear of that restless imagined predator.

We all did our buddy-check: buoyancy, regulator, weights, air, and final check. We climbed down the rocks and eased into the Pacific. The water was murky and dark. The posts of the piers were overgrown with long green algae that danced in the current, which pulled us out from the cove, carrying me away, past the pier and the rippled sand bar into the pale green water. When I checked my gauges, I was surprised to see we were already at thirty-five feet.

"*Okay?*" signaled the instructor.

"*I'm okay,*" Chris signaled.

"*I'm okay,*" I signaled.

Neon purple and yellow fish swam by. I was suspended between the surface and the bottom where the water was as warm as a womb. The current rocked me, and as far as I could see there were rippling flats of sand and clear water. A small school swam under us; they were black with white polka-dots. The smallest one in the bunch had light-colored eyes. He seemed so curious but calm and as we swam and hovered over him he just looked at me as if, weirdly, he was checking us out as much as we were him. I could hear my breath sucking in deeply and gurgling out through the regulator. It sounded like the respirators in an NICU. Being underwater, under pressure, created a measurable aware-ness that at any given moment we could stop breathing. I checked my air gauge. It was half full. Below my feet an enormous conch shell rested on the ocean floor. Here on the ocean floor, as low as I could go, was a symbol of the truth of Dharma that spreads in all directions like the sound of a conch horn blaring.

THE NEXT DAY off a sandy shore we walked straight into the sea. The water was clear: cyan, azure, and sapphire, baby blue, sky blue, Blue Poppy blue. We went to forty-seven feet.

"*Look that way,*" signaled the instructor.

A giant turtle was swimming toward Chris and me. I was transfixed for a minute until I realized the turtle was not going to stop. I looked at Chris; his eyes were as big as sand dollars.

I signaled, "*Get with your buddy.*"

"*Hold hands,*" signaled Chris.

We got out of the way as the turtle, which must have been four feet in diameter, glided by. There was only a small space between us. He was old; I'm sure he had seen many people—all kinds of creatures—pass.

I could have stayed underwater forever. In some ways, over the next few months, and the years beyond our global sojourn, I did. Those diving lessons served us well in the next nearly three months while we were submerged in sadness and travel. Chris and I had little need for words. We signaled to each other in a world full of signs, looking—hoping—for a small amount, if only the size of a mustard seed, of comfort.

IN THE TIME OF THE BUDDHA, a young mother's son became very ill and died. She was overcome with grief. She went to the Buddha and asked him to bring her son back to life. He said he would help her, but first she had to bring him a mustard seed from the home of a person who had never known anyone who died. She had hope and set off. She searched through many villages and for a long time no one could give her what she thought she needed. Finally she found what the Buddha had really sent her to find, the truth that he was trying to teach her: the truth that she wasn't alone in her suffering, that death comes to everyone. She brought her son's body to the charnel ground and let him go. She returned to the Buddha and told him that she had found the real cure that he was offering her and asked him to be her teacher.

As Chris and I set off for Southeast Asia and the land of the Buddha after our short campout on the shore of our past, I wondered what I would find. I wondered if I would be able to let go. I wondered if the truth that the Buddha taught would be enough to help me. I was in search not of the reason why, but of the reason why not. Why not give up if life is only suffering?

A Place Dense with Memory

About suffering they were never wrong,
The Old Masters; how well, they understood
Its human position; how it takes place
While someone else is eating or opening a window or just
walking dully along . . .
—*W.H. Auden*

A N OLD FRIEND FROM COLLEGE, Jim, met us off the
plane.

From the window of his apartment in "Happy Valley" (as
it translates), Hong Kong, I saw an old woman across Wong Nai
Chung Road come out onto her narrow balcony. In its corner was a
shrine, a red-and-yellow wood box with a scalloped border, three
joss sticks in a bowl of rice, and fruit piled on a gold tray for offerings. As she prostrated, the images and statues of deities on her altar
accepted her offering of clasped hands pressed to her forehead,
then throat, then heart, purifying and dedicating her body, speech,
and mind. She bowed down onto her knees; heels of hands hit concrete and slid forward to lay her body out in full prostration. Her

hands punctuated the gesture as they came together again and flared up above her head just like the flames that gave way and righted themselves again inside the red rice-paper lanterns on her shrine.

AFTER LIAM PASSED, a shrine grew on our living room table. Spontaneously, things pilled up there: pictures and cards and prayer flags; roses and candles, phenobarbital bottles and a stethoscope; *Ferdinand the Bull*, a story about an animal who prefers flowers to fighting; a *thangka* painting of Padmapani Avalokiteshvara, from whose tears of compassion were born Green and White Tara, the female forms of the bodhisattva of compassion and mercy; and a small wooden box that holds a lock of Liam's hair, the shirt he was wearing when he died, and a tiny heart-shaped shell I found on the shore soon after he was gone and I was walking and missing him.

I WAS FAMILIAR with this Buddhist ritual of prostration that the women on the balcony offered before her shrine. A memory of the old woman's gesture was embedded in my body too. As she gave in and dropped to her knees over and over, I too felt the comfortable surrender of prostration that offers, in return, a connection to the ideas, buddhas, and people symbolically present on the shrine one bows before and venerates. In a prostration we lay down our egos, who we believe ourselves to be, and we sit with a spacious mind and find out who we really are. We were separated by the gaping abyss between our two buildings, a thin pane of glass, and a whole culture—yet the ritual she performed to surrender self-grasping, focus the mind, and extract meaning from the long day was my ritual too.

...

THERE WERE OTHER ROUTINES that salted our days and nourished our questions.

Every morning, in the restaurant on the ground floor of the building across the street, Chris and I stopped to buy breakfast from the Steamed-Bun Man. Puffs of dough, called *bao*, that were slightly tacky to the touch and filled with savory or sweet fillings, were displayed at counter level behind a window that slid open on the far side. My favorite was the sweet pork. It was sinewy, but the bland dough was soft on my tongue.

The Bun Man, with a face as round as his *bao*, leaned forward with his palms on the glass counter, elbows locked, shoulders squared, and jutted his chin once in my direction. I pointed to my favorite buns and held up two fingers. His chin jutted to Chris. I pointed at two red-bean buns for him. The Bun Man put the warm puffs in a small white bag as I dug forty *yuan* from my coin purse.

"*Shey-shey,*" I thanked him, taking the bag. I think I saw the thought of a smile pass over his eyes, but it didn't make it to his lips. I munched my breakfast buns as Chris and I walked down the block to the trolley stop on the left side of the Hong Kong Jockey Club's racecourse. The green double-decker bus was already at the stop. We hopped on and waited for it to fill with passengers. I wasn't sure we were on the right trolley and neither of us could ask anyone because we didn't speak Mandarin (or Cantonese for that matter), but I hoped we were headed in the right direction.

In the belly of the trolley we moved along the tracks. We rounded the Polo Club and slid under the elevated highway, which rose to reveal a slice of a Christian cemetery—a small lot of crosses. The Hong Kong air sweltered in a world laden with ghosts. Just beneath the surface, ancestors and ritual pushed up against the weight of modernization like unseen corpses forcing headstones askew.

Next to the concrete pillar that held up the highway, the sidewalk ended and a person lay there in a cot with a green, dingy blanket pulled over their head. Next to the bed sat a box and on it sat a pan, dentures, and a pair of eyeglasses with its arms reaching out. Though the owner of the spectacles was hidden away from my view, that simple object, the lens through which another unfortunate person views the world, reached out to me. I craned my neck as we rolled by, unable to drop the surprising hold that witnessing someone else's suffering had on me. Finally I turned around in my seat, not knowing what I could do even if I could stop the bus and get off. How does a person end up living in a house with walls made of peering eyes and car exhaust? Are all our walls so transparent? Could everyone on that bus see my walls that were made of baby cribs empty except for blankets of yellow flannel and rainbow silk, tiny oral syringes for phenobarbital, vacant breasts, and books on how to birth "the right way" but not what to do when everything goes so wrong?

WE GOT OFF THE TROLLEY and negotiated the streets—clotted with people of all nationalities—to the Chinese consulate. We needed to apply for our visas to Mainland China where we planned to continue our journey overland to Tibet. Since the borders to Tibet opened, it had become easier to get a visa to go there. But the Chinese officials were unpredictable; it was always possible to be denied entrance to the country of which they have so savagely taken possession. The visa office was not yet open when we arrived, so we waited in the line that had already formed. At the front of the line, the woman behind the counter, stone-faced as a temple lion, pointed again and again to a sign, which read, "Due to rules of reciprocity, those holding American passports must pay $160 more." She barked some directions batting us aside with her hand. Pay or move on was the message we inferred. We did move on since we didn't have enough money with us to acquiesce to the state's demand, and she didn't care when we pointed to a sign that stated a different price altogether for the same visa.

Deflated, we walked back through Victoria Park to the busy market district of Central. Great George Street melted into Hennessy Road, and into Yee Woo Street, which ran parallel to Hysan Avenue, and Caroline Hill Road. All those streets with their Chinese names were the putty that held together the tiles of the colonial city-blocks and buildings that were reclaimed by China from Great Britain just one year before. I wondered how Hong Kong would change under Chinese rule. Amidst monolithic skyscrapers, shrines to modernity and white devils, the ancient and appropriate shrines were low to the ground; stout red-tiled roofs sat low, like the brims of the fishermen's hats, and weighted the culture down so the spirit of the place wouldn't leach away.

The Mid-Escalators of Central is the world's longest covered outdoor escalator system: 800 meters long with a vertical climb of 135 meters. Incrementally, there are landings where a person can get on or off to shop or eat in one of the restaurants lining the steep street. As we rode the giant escalator I could see on the streets below a stream of people and activity. Joss sticks burned slow and bright in storefront shrines. Tea-smoked ducks and pig's hooves were tethered and hung in rows above steaming bamboo baskets of rice. Butchers in bloody aprons pushed wheelbarrows with pigs splayed out, disemboweled, snouts trickling blood, eyes open. Eels entwined each other, a quivering dark weave within the pale wicker basket that contained them. Carp and trout crowded tanks that crowded a fish stall big enough for only one woman, whose skin was smoked and taut with age; she netted a catch for the customer, a woman reed-like with black, silky hair, who pointed into the dark stall. The child on her hip with moonlight skin and midnight hair pointed up to me as I passed overhead on the escalator. His black lacquer eyes met my pale blue ones.

Liam's eyes had not settled in color; sometimes they were sapphire, at times onyx and vacant, at other times wise with more presence than I have ever known. They spoke to me about impermanence, told me that everyone suffers, not just him and me and Chris, and about how when he passed, if I could remember to let compassion guide me, humility hold me, and courage temper my wild mind, then he would never be gone from me.

At the end of his life when his breath was still, his eyes were wide open.

IN MY MIND, I reached through the air thick with Hong Kong's heat and spice to touch that moonlight-midnight baby's outstretched finger with the tip of my own and smiled. I was grateful for the touch of his attention, though he was too far away to reach.

At the top of the escalators, Chris and I wound back down the narrow streets with trolley tracks running up and down like spines. The sidewalks were steep with steps, every step an effort. We were looking for the temple of Guanyin, the bodhisattva of compassion who is also the protector of those gone to sea or lost there. I was hoping to make an offering additional to that of our son's ashes in the ocean at home: of my tears that came in waves. In temples all over like these, old women prostrated themselves each day before ancestral altars, the weight of their ritual a spiritual anchor in a changing time.

On narrow side streets we trolled the antique stalls filled with ivory chops and lacquer boxes. I was drawn to a stand of jade bracelets like the ones that adorned the wrists of Hong Kong's women and girls. Milky green and cold, I also wanted to force a ring of stone that symbolized luck over my large hand so it wouldn't come off. The Buddha said that the likelihood of being born into the auspicious life of a human was as likely as a turtle that surfaces only once every hundred years, popping its head up through a ring that happens to be floating on the ocean. I wanted a round jade bangle to remind me of this precious human existence. I wanted good luck. I took a picture of the stall instead of buying a bracelet because Chris was worried about spending money so early in the trip. I agreed, figuring it a good exercise of nonattachment. A picture would allow me to have and not have it, and maybe protect me from feeling bad if I should some day lose it.

We didn't find the temple of Guanyin, but found instead the Man Mo Temple. Man is the deity of literature, and Mo is the deity of the art of war, who's also the patron saint of tradesmen and professionals. Huge coils of smoking incense, spirit food to keep ancestors happy, hung inside the dark temple. Lighting an offering there is said to make your wish come true. Though I looked for a sign from the bodhisattva of compassion and guardian of those traveling on the unpredictable sea, I found symbols of words and struggle from the deity of literature and the protector of common people. Golden cauldrons rested on pedestals of lions' paws were full of incense ash. New sticks, some as thick and long as bamboo poles, some slender as chopsticks, were planted in the burned remains of previous offerings—a smoking, ash garden of gratitude and desire. I also bought incense and planted my offerings and wishes, repeating the invocation, "May we all have happiness, and may we all be free from suffering without too much attachment and too much aversion."

On our way back to Happy Valley we came across a tourist agency. We were thrilled when we asked for visas to Mainland China and weren't required to pay $160 extra. We were told to leave our passports and come back in two days to pick up our visas.

...

THE NEXT DAY was Halloween, and when we woke I felt like doing something to observe the day even though it meant very little in China except to the expatriates. When we were out buying buns I bought offerings for a day-of-the-dead altar for Liam: pastel lollipops, incense, a small candle, and a miniature bottle of milk. Halloween was my favorite holiday and in the past I savored the Mexican and Celtic rituals of putting out offerings for the dead. It's said that the spirits of the children arrive beginning at midnight on the thirtieth. I never thought my son would be one of them, and I made the small altar more solemnly than ever before. Tradition says that on the night of Halloween the veil between the living and the dead is at its thinnest. I'm not sure if what I wanted was to be closer to my dead son on that day, or to be dead myself.

"What should Liam be for Halloween?" I asked Chris.

"How about a duck?"

We talked about a lamb and a pea-in-a-pod. We decided on a lion. The sound of the Dharma, the Buddha's teachings, is like the roar of a lion. We pretended we would buy a little mustard-yellow sweat suit and socks for his feet and hands. I would sew brownish-red yarn all around the rim of the hood and small patches of felt on the socks to make the paws, a little black facepaint on his nose and some whiskers. The colors would have looked so nice with his honey-red hair—our little lion who was teaching us about courage.

I laid out the offerings on the nightstand. Chris and I sat together, lit the candle and incense, and were silent for some time in meditation.

Later that night, Jim's roommate came home to fix himself some sausages and mac-and-cheese before he went out to a Halloween party in Central with a group of other twenty-three-year-old expats. He had just taken the Associated Press journalist credentialing exam. "I don't know if I'll use the credentials," he said, taking off his tie and jacket, draping them over the back of a chair, "but it's good to have options. So what's your five-year plan?"

Chris and I both laughed because we didn't realize at first that he was serious. There was a silence as he waited for our answers.

"Well," I said, "I had planned to stay home and raise my son. But there's been an obvious change to that. So, now I don't know what I'm going to do beyond this trip."

"Oh, sorry, I forgot," he paused, looking out the window. "You guys want some sausage? Help yourself to some tea."

I felt bad and was shocked by my stark answer. I was tired and my sharp thoughts were on my tongue before I could soften them. And I guess I envied his options and success, feeling like a failure myself and knowing the one thing I wanted was not an option. "No, thanks," I declined. "We just had rice and sweet short-ribs from the vendor on the corner. Greasy, but good."

"Yeah," Chris finally answered the first question, "I don't know what I'm gonna do."

"Yes, you do, Chris. You're going to go to grad school when we get back. It will take five years to finish your doctorate in psychology."

"Yeah, I guess I do have a plan."

I sat on the couch and turned on CNN. Bill Clinton wagged his finger—"I never . . ."—stock prices, weather, peace talks. Jim's roommate headed to the door, having already changed his clothes, with his mask in hand. "You guys don't want to come, do you?"

"Oh, no, thanks, but have fun."

I flicked through the channels: Japanese game shows, Chinese commercials for dish soap, kung fu movies that weren't dubbed——the actors' mouths in sync with the words for a change. We settled on *The Bride of Frankenstein*. Black-and-white, shadows, thunderclaps, a shock of white hair with a black lightning bolt through it—in a gossamer white gown, she made a startling bride.

Even monsters can love, need love. I felt like a monster for not implementing any heroic measures to try to extend Liam's life. That night in bed, while the veil between life and death was sheerest, in half-waking dreams of our own, Chris and I found each other and came to full wakefulness in the midst of a deep kiss, tongues and limbs intertwined, the sound of soft skin rubbing against soft skin filled our dark room. The closer we were to death, I think, the closer we instinctively reached for life. Maybe that's what we all do. Maybe that's why our attachments in this life are so strong, because we instinctively know how close we are to death even though we don't always perceive it, or can't always utter the unspeakable truth of it. I want to believe accepting that truth can endow a rare blessing if we're open to a different view of grief and hardship.

WE FILLED OUR DAYS waiting for visas with side-trips around Hong Kong. We took the trolley to Causeway Bay to catch the ferry to Lantau Island. It was early and a few fishing junks dwarfed by the ferries and container ships were just heading out. The hulls of the junks' thick beams were as dark as tea leaves. The square, red sails filled with the South China Sea's breeze.

A fisherman squinting even under the protection of his straw hat lowered the fan rudder off the back, and with the long wooden handle turned the rudder to coax the bow of his junk out to open sea. The woman—in a suit to match his blue, padded, Mandarin-collared jacket, blue cotton pants, and black cloth shoes—gathered a hulking net from the deck, a matrix of yellowing ropes as thick and worn as her wrists. Bits of cork every few feet on the net kept it from sinking too fast under its own weight when she threw it from the side of the boat. Her body glided, though the weight was great, like a tai chi–master's movements in the park: plant the foot, heart balanced, knees over ankles, snap the wrist, hold the peacock by the tail, close the door. As the net hit the water, her eyes landed on me just as the lens of the camera that I was looking through came down before my eye. I was surprised by the smile that bloomed wide—a brilliant white across her face stained teak by the hard days of sun and salt, wave and balance, cast and pull, endlessly dragging the pale bright waters for small fish of flesh and thin bones to fill the belly, sell, or trade for greens in the market. She waved to me and I to her after the shutter sounded.

We watched from the stern of the Starr Ferry as Hong Kong faded away and we headed for Discovery Bay on Lantau Island. The breeze was cool. The China Sea was almost as blue as the Pacific shores of Hawaii. Once we reached the island we followed the tourist crowd to the bus marked Po Lin Monastery, where the thousand-foot-tall *Tin Tan* Buddha sat—a mountain-like emblem of the Dharma, rendered in bronze. The bus took us along the southern coast, and once we rounded Lantau Peak, even from miles away, as our bus turned inland and we drew nearer, we could see the head of the Buddha dawning over the mountains.

We made our way past the trinket stalls selling jade Buddha pendants, small strings of mala beads to wear on the wrist, crystal and gold statues of Guanyin, piles of incense wrapped in red, yellow, and pink cellophane. I bought three foot-long sticks of juniper incense to make an offering in memory of Liam.

Once we passed the monastery gates at the far side of the entry courtyard, the hawking and pervasive sound of the shrill Chinese songs playing incessantly from the speakers of the stalls dissipated like the incense smoke rising from the huge cast-iron cauldrons. The smoke was so thick it was tangible. I gathered a cloud of it in my first, then let it go. Hundreds of ornate iron boxes held thousands of burning red candles; their smoke was black and blended with the white smoke of the offering incense that rose up until it lost form and became the air all around. There was no answer. There was no question. There was just ritual, smoke, music, and native strangers all around me. Standing before the Tin Tan Buddha, he gave no answers, but silently offered me an outstretched hand and downcast eyes.

Borrowed-Bones Boxes and Wide-Heart Doors

I'm worn and I'm happy 'cause I've never forgot,
these bones are borrowed, oh, but this heart is not.
—*Kate Klim*

OUR HOSPICE NURSE CAME INTO THE ROOM where I sat on the bed with Liam. She hugged me, and then slid Liam's rigid body toward her. She held Liam folded in her arms and ran a finger from his temple to under his chin.

"Hi, Liam," she said. I thought she was really saying goodbye but wanted to be cautious of my feelings in case I was not ready to hear that.

She was going to drive us to the funeral home. Chris wrapped Liam in the hand-stitched white quilt with the little black Scotty dogs on it that he received in the NICU. Chris carried Liam from the bedroom. Before he went through the front door, he poked his head out a bit, looked side-to-side, and back over his shoulder to me.

"I just want to make sure there are no neighbors coming," he said. We focused on the car and walked straight to it. We didn't want anyone to intrude on the last moments we had with our son. We dreaded getting caught having to attempt chitchat, or, worse yet, seeing the look on a neighbor's face as they realized Chris was holding our dead baby. If it was cold or mild out, I didn't notice.

Sitting in the back seat we were enveloped in the scent of smoke that rose like an apparition all around us. Sharon always sat in her car and had a cigarette while she made her notes when she left our house. I'd watched her through the window. How many cigarettes did she smoke a day? How many children did she visit? How many small lives were smoldering down?

Hawthorne Street was empty as we drove down ten blocks to Holman's Funeral Home. Funny how funeral homes are usually the biggest, nicest houses on the block but no one lives there. The front door was heavy and wide enough for three people abreast to walk through, though most likely only two of them would be walking.

It was quiet inside—warm and neutered of scent, the opposite of death. Liam's body smelled like wipey-dipes and renal failure, sticky-sweet phenobarbital and Baby Magic Shampoo. Cold seemed to radiate from his body. But in contrast, strangely, his hair still felt warm and soft to me.

The carpet was red and thin. The pews in the chapel were brown, and bare, and silent.

A woman came out of the office to greet us. Her tone of voice was hushed. I wondered whom she was trying not to disturb. Her eyes weighed on me like an arm around my shoulder, and she led us down the thick hall. I became hushed too and felt like I was tiptoe-ing through a nightmare.

"Have a seat." The mortician gestured with an open palm to the two chairs in front of his square, brown desk. There were no pictures on the walls. There was a large window behind him, and I watched the roof of a bus pass the front hedge. I remembered a mortician telling me once that by law a funeral must be blocked from the view of people passing by. Before the mortician sat he leaned toward Liam in Chris's arms.

"Do you want me to take the baby now?"

"No, not yet," Chris answered, taking a seat.

No wake. No service. We had no strength to plan and go through any of those rituals. We decided on cremation.

"Where will you do the cremation? Will you do it here?" I asked.

"No. He'll . . . is it a boy?" he asked.

"Yes." We both nodded.

"He'll be taken by car to the crematorium in South-West."

I clenched my eyes and fought away the image of Liam in a stranger's car alone. I knew the place to which the mortician was referring. It was on the hill near Lewis & Clark College, from where I had graduated eight years before. Out in front of that crematorium I had picked up Chris, who was hitchhiking home from a party one morning. He later told me he had stayed so late, hoping I would show up to the party when I got off work, that he had to stay overnight there.

"Should we have them wait three days to cremate him?" I asked Chris.

"I don't know."

"In the Buddhist tradition," I explain to the mortician, "the body is not moved for three days so the consciousness has a chance to leave the body."

"Sure," he said, nodding, not moving, even his eyes blinked slowly and solemnly, "that's not a problem."

"Where would you keep him?" I asked.

"Downstairs in the basement."

Chris and I looked at each other and down at Liam.

"I don't want him to be alone for three days," I said.

"Me neither. That sort of defeats the purpose, I think," Chris said.

Cremation. As soon as possible was what we decided. We wrote the check for $75, which was the special low-price, I was told, that they standardly charge for a child's cremation. It comforted me a bit to think they knew parents in need of their services had already paid the very dearest price of our lives. The fact that they had a "standard" price told me there are more children dying than anyone ever knows. We were now part of a community that has no name, that no one asks to be a part of, and that most people never and don't want to think about. The mortician stood and reached out for Liam as he rounded the desk toward us. We didn't move. The mortician retracted his arms.

"Do you need some more time with him?"

"Yes," I said, and I thought, *Can you give me a lifetime?*

We all left his office and headed back down the hall past the casket display room, the living-room-ish room, and the chapel-ish room. Rooms to reflect personality. Rooms to reflect value and meaning. Is the body a room for our spirit? Is it a flesh-and-bone motel? How do we make reservations for the next lifetime? Who takes the complaints when we don't get the room we want? How do I make reservations for a happily-ever-after because this was not the life I booked?

I'd made different plans for this trip. I did the Bradley birthing classes. I didn't smoke or drink. I ate right and did prenatal yoga. Chris gave me massages and went to every prenatal checkup with me. I swam three times a week, took vitamins, went on maternity leave early when I had a preterm labor scare. This was not how my "birthing story" was supposed to end. The mortician closed the door behind him, leaving us in the room at the end of the hall. The window shades were pulled down, and the yellow light of the lamp oozed from either end of the cylindrical shade.

Putting one arm around Chris's shoulder, I joined him on the twill couch and placed my free hand under his arms that were full of Liam. Chris told Liam how proud he was to be his father, that he'd never be forgotten, and thanked him for being his baby. Tears ran. My eyes burned. Chris's eyes were red and puffy, too. I took a deep breath, and I reached out to take Liam from Chris's arms.

"I need to hold him one more time, one last time." I felt my milk let down as I took him to my chest. "Liam, I know I have to let you go. I love you. You're my honey little Buddha boy. You're the best baby in the world. I know this is just your body, so I can leave you here and you'll always be with me. I'm sorry this body was so bad for you. Next time you'll have the body you need." I planted my lips on his cold forehead, kissing him. I breathed in.

The door opened.

"Excuse me," the mortician said. He was slightly stooped as he entered the room. "I don't want to interrupt. I just thought you might like to put him in this yourself." With one hand he held out a white cardboard box no bigger than one that might hold a new-bought doll.

I swallowed my heart and hugged Liam closer to my breasts, swelling and hot with milk.

"I can't do it, Chris," I said, turning to him. I wasn't strong enough to carry around for the rest of my life the image of Liam in a small box.

"It's okay," Chris said, wrapping his arm around my shoulder and laying his free hand under Liam, never taking his eyes off him. "I'll do it." His voice was like a wave, soothing and strong. Chris lifted Liam from my arms. I was still seated and turned toward the now closed door.

"Okay," Chris said, and I rose without looking at them. I felt Chris's weight lift up from the couch where we left Liam's borrowed bones in a box. We reached the door just as the mortician was coming through it again.

"I just wanted to give you this. Oh . . ." he saw Liam was already in the box. The mortician was holding a small white ceramic heart on a gold string. The inside of the heart was cut away from the outer edge creating a smaller heart inside the frame of a bigger heart. "Some people like to put the smaller heart with the baby and keep the outer heart with them. So your heart can go with your baby and symbolize how your heart will always be empty from now on." The mortician backed out the door again.

"That's the saddest thing I've ever heard," I said, and Chris agreed.

We decided without further discussion. We would try to leave our fragile hearts full. I put the clay heart, whole, into my pocket.

In a few steps we were halfway to the wide front door that the three of us had walked through together. By reflex I turned back for Liam. The door to the room we left Liam in was closed already. I couldn't go back. I froze. I felt like I couldn't go forward without him either. I told myself again that it was just his body; Liam was already somewhere else; I wasn't leaving him there. I clutched my chest. My heart was rendered wide open. My breasts were still tender. I turned back to the wide-open door, took Chris's hand and walked. Liam's body was behind me, but his face was all I could see the whole drive home.

The house, so quiet and empty, seemed to be holding its breath too. I picked up the phone and dialed.

"Hello."

"Mom," I said. She knew by the tone in my voice, but just in case it might make it more believable to me, I said it anyway.

Grim Poetry Bears Birthing and the Dead

The tears of the world are a constant quality. For each one
who begins to weep, somewhere else another stops.
The same is true of the laugh.
—*Samuel Beckett*

ROM HONG KONG'S HUNG HOM STATION in
Kowloon we took the High Speed Express Through Train
to Guangzhou East Station on Mainland China. On the
advice of Jim's friend, who had traveled extensively in China, we
headed to Saimen Island in Guangzhou. "Guangzhou is a
cesspool," he said. "I love it. But if you're only staying a night, the
Saimen International Guest House is the only place to stay. It's clean
and cheap." He added, "And be careful at the station; it's a den of
thieves."

So, four days before my twenty-eighth birthday, Chris and I
arrived in the "Motherland," another name for Mainland China
found in political propaganda after 1949. I was now a mother only

in theory; Chris was a father only in his heart. We found our way by map and luck to the recommended accommodations. As we paid for a room, we asked about train tickets to Chengdu, which was a city to the north of Guangzhou. It was the next stop on our route to Tibet. We were told we wouldn't be able to get a ticket for a couple of days and they'd be happy to buy the tickets for us for 600 yuan. We declined the offer, took the key, and headed to our room to store our packs before we went out to investigate our options for dinner and purchasing train tickets.

We found another hotel with a ubiquitous travel agency in the lobby. The young woman was stoic as we tried to negotiate a ticket sounding out certain words in our guidebook's dictionary and pointing to them when that failed: train, Chengdu, Wednesday, hard berth, top bunk. We used a calculator to dicker for price, 458 yuan. We made an agreement, and she conveyed the message with fingers pointed at her watch and waving hands that we would have to come back at 9:30 that night to pick up our tickets. At least that's what we hoped we'd settled on.

We strolled through the streets. Guangzhou was an anomaly. Its white stone buildings were built in an English style since it once was the English section of town where all the diplomats and dignitaries and their families had once lived. Now its white paved streets were peppered with traditional market stalls: snakes, greens, turtles, radishes, dogs, tomatoes, bean curd, sprouts. We stopped at a restaurant that had outdoor tables and managed to order tall Singha beers, which were cheaper than buying water. We were happy to be at rest and watch Guangzhou stroll by us.

Guangzhou was also, we deduced, a town where foreigners came to adopt their Chinese babies. Before we were halfway through our Singhas, I had counted seven European couples with a Chinese baby. Two more had passed by the time we were given our menus just a few minutes later. We amused ourselves perusing a menu that read like a zoological list mixed with a botanical encyclopedia truncated to poetic phrases.

Westerners, with smiles as long as the Yangtze, strolled the town with their new Chinese children who had basalt hair and dark eyes that peeked out of NoJo baby slings while their new parents bought for them tiny brocade jackets and embroidered slippers. I wanted to buy them all dainty jade bracelets and slip them over their small hands before their fists grew too big and different. Perhaps only months before they had lost their parents. Maybe they only had had a mother to lose. Perhaps it was only yesterday they had crossed the bridge to Saimen Island and lost sight of the part of Guangzhou that wasn't anglicized and already foreign. Soon those surrendered children would cross an ocean just as we had. We and those children had something in common: someone was missing, and someone was surrendered to a better place. Chris and I held hands. Neither of us talked but craned our necks to count all the babies around us that were not ours. Would they know what they had to let go of in order to be carried into their future? Would they know the ones who let them go still carry the pain of that rend, and love them?

In my mind the strange concoctions of families on parade and the dishes on the menu mixed together as I read and watched. Spring greens delight. Fat, red mom with tall, blond dad and moon-face baby with a dark cloud of hair above. Forest mushrooms with snake in black bean sauce. Tall dad with short dad and baby with a pearl face and porcelain hands. Whole duck roasted with oranges and cashew. Brown mom with gray dad and baby in the pram like a precious offering of a peony. Salt and pepper long beans with crispy young dog. Round, bald dad and slender, blonde mom with baby wished for and destined to be loved like a discovered treasure. Fried pig brains and medicinal materials in casserole.

Our baby too was wished for, though his karma and ours meant his life had passed like a flame running over a match-stick in my fingers, burning fast, and bright, touching me for a brief intense moment before I was forced to let go, and stand in the dark, blistered and wounded. We were left to pull together answers from myth and earth, feet blistered from walking and wounded souls, to press meaning from the fullness of his time with us like carbon is pressed to a diamond. Happy Family. Buddha's Delight. I wished we could place an order for my son to be healthy and whole and with us again. I wished I could place an order for a happy ending, like those adoptive parents had.

Chris and I did experience moments of relief evoked from the strangeness around us. We relished a light moment together at the table laughing because some of the dishes seemed so unusual and even grotesque to our Western sensibilities. But there was something ironic in the menu's offerings. Some of the ingredients were grim, but there was poetry in their phrasing. Some ingredients of Liam's life were grim at best—brain-damage most likely caused by a massive blood clot in his heart—but there was something poignant and beautiful to savor in the days he was with us. The laughter, the days with Liam, would nourish us to struggle through the next inevitable fight over directions and train schedules and desired destinations, and the times when Chris and I would be of no use to each other in that deep-end of loss and despair, because when I looked at his face, and he at mine, all we saw was Liam.

When our meal arrived, the bean curd and straw mushrooms were silken and savory on our tongues. We continued to admire the parade of new families. Our eyes were filled with other people's joy. With the soft touch of our hands, his pouring of tea into my empty cup, my gesture to him to eat the last of the curd and rice, I tried to hold on to our happiness. Silence and space, the night unbidden, touch and words created the maze of our days as we made our way around the world, by meal, by train, by shrine, by fight, by plane, by kiss, country to country.

At 9:30 PM we returned to the agent and picked up our tickets. After matching each character on the ticket to the character in the guidebook, we believed we got the tickets we wanted: Guangzhou to Chengdu, top bunk, hard berth, Nov. 5, 10:10 AM.

Sometimes what we think we want is really worse than what was meant to be. Life, in some cases, may be worse than death.

We opted for a cab to the train station rather than taking the chance of finding our way on the bus. Our light skin was a magnet for all the dark eyes in the station. We were the only Westerners in sight. It was harder and harder for me to breathe as I felt the hundreds and hundreds of eyes groping my body and squeezing the breath out of me. They robbed my peace of mind. I snapped at Chris to figure out where we were supposed to get on the train in the maze of the station with signs all around us written in strange characters. I stifled an urge to run, knowing there was nowhere to run to. I found a less crowded corner and sat on my pack. Pulling my skirt hem over my toes I folded over my bent legs and hid my breasts. I embraced my knees with my arms and made a hole in which I hid my head. I could feel my blood rushing. I wanted to puke. My face was numb and tingling.

When I looked up, there was a group of seven men who had formed a semi-circle around me not four feet away; they stared lasciviously and dragged slowly on cigarettes exhaling with open mouths. Two of them had crossed arms and squinted down at me, one was actually squatting on his haunches too close to me. My stomach turned and quickly I was on my feet and hauling my pack over my shoulder.

"Where are you going?" My sudden movement startled Chris

who, still sitting, had joined me though I didn't notice when. "I can't stand this. What are we doing? What are we *doing*?" I focused on my dirty toes in my black sandals. Everyone was staring at us.

"What's wrong with you?" Though not oblivious to the stares, Chris seemed unaffected by them.

"What do you think?" I barked and moved toward a seat next to two women. They stared too, but I read only interest and disgust in their eyes, and I was less frightened.

After I calmed a bit we started to wonder again if we were in the right place. We showed our tickets to a conductor. With a sneer she waved us to the far side of the room. Again we made our way to the other side of the room. The throng had begun to shuffle en masse toward the black metal gate that blocked the opening to a tunnel. We joined the mass with our packs on our backs.

"What's going on?" I asked Chris. We looked at our tickets again, and they didn't make any more sense to us than they did a few minutes before. We were pushed and nudged. We planted our feet and tried to stay shoulder to shoulder. I was grateful for the extra foot of height I had over the crowd. Together we swayed, clotted together like the body of a jellyfish. Chris and I were pushed up against the people in front of us, who were pushed against more people, who were pushed and doubled over the gate. Just as I began to worry that they'd be crushed if the gate didn't open, it did and the crowd disgorged. A small woman in front of me began to fall. I grabbed her arm so she wouldn't go down as the people flushed around us like blood rushing through a vein. She righted herself without looking at me and flew into the tunnel, a small mass breaking away from a clot.

The doctors believed that a blood clot in Liam's heart broke away and went to his brain, cutting off his oxygen, and damaging 80 percent of it.

We ran too, not knowing why. Our feet slapped the concrete. The sound bounced off the cement walls and was absorbed into the gurgle of Chinese phrases and shouts from our fellow passengers that were so unintelligible to my ears it might as well have been a symphony, the dip and treble of the language sounded like a musical phrase, that sound of so many voices uttering words I didn't understand. Yet I knew there was meaning. I felt their words around me. I knew they said, "Run," though we all knew exactly what seat we would take in the end. I knew they said, "Hurry," though the train had just pulled in. I knew they said, "I'm coming, go ahead," as they waddle-ran through the tunnel, loose blue cotton pants and jackets concealing the strain of their muscles as they hefted their luggage—square, plastic bags almost as big as their bodies. Chris and I ran, too, loads on our backs.

"Why are we running?" I called to Chris.

"This is crazy," he yelled back. "Which way do we go?"

"Follow me," I signaled.

All the while the din around us swelled to the final crescendo.

LIAM'S VOICE was mostly silent. We spoke with our hearts. His voice was suffocated when, sometime in the dark warmth of my womb, his oxygen was cut off. Later, only when he was having a seizure did he make a sound, that unmistakable tragic sound of a brain-damaged baby. A sharp twisted whine like the sound a burning violin would make if the flames dissolving the catgut could sustain a note and play out a song instead of devouring it. Once, Liam cried, at a week old, when we were leaving the hospital. Once, he shrieked when a fat, insensitive nurse ripped tape from his cheek. But he never cried for food, he never shrieked when he was stuck with needles to draw quarts of blood, or to start IV lines to replace fluids and drip drugs to keep his heart pumping, or run in radioactive fluids to take images of his brain.

WE ARRIVED on the platform, having emerged from the tunnel up a flight of stairs. The dark shiny flow of people moved past us and onto the train. On the car's iron side there was a plaque and our heads bobbed from ticket to plaque as we matched the characters written there line-by-line to make sure that it said Chengdu and car eight.

The ubiquitous music in the car—a mix of Cantonese pop and Motherland-nationalist songs—was already playing. Everywhere we went in China there was music. Not music in an uplifting, the-hills-are-alive way, but driving, prying songs, songs that seemed to eavesdrop on my solitude and spy on my thoughts. As we rode for fifty hours in the belly of the train that crawled its way across lower China, I felt I would slowly suffocate.

The car was narrow. The windows that didn't open looked out to the platform, then to the passing station, and then to the rice fields that flew by. The scratched fuzzy glass was clear as fog and made the dried bamboo-like faces of the farmers and reedy terraced fields seem even more dreamlike—even though I couldn't dream, or sleep, or breathe, or cry, or talk, or move for fear I'd be chipped away by the eye-grip of the passengers' stares that were always on me, the bloated pale oddity. I couldn't walk the length of the car because the passage was clogged with men standing to pass the time. When necessity made me take the trip down to the car to the toilet, I held my breath with eyes cast down as I tried to slide past strangers in a space not much wider than my own breadth as we all rattled and clanked, rattled and clanked, down the line, reaching out when possible for balance.

When I reached the toilet, the tracks blurred under the hole in the floor of the metal room that was no wider than a gurney, which bears the weight of the birthing and the dead. Gut twisting painfully, I lifted my skirt and hoped the cramp in my stomach was from the need for an urgent evacuation and not the beginning of a more severe and dreaded disorder. The breeze cooled my bottom, and I rested my forehead on my knees. Even in that uncomfortable and vulnerable position, I was grateful to be alone in my bare loneliness for a few minutes. Perhaps the way I felt trapped in that train unable to control my own bodily functions was how Liam might have felt trapped in his own unresponsive body.

Making my way back down the aisle, I saw people had changed into pajamas and slippers, unpacked thermoses of tea, and laid out fruit on the small tables between the bunks. Our bunkmates on the lower and middle berths were also settled nicely. A relaxed grandma stretched out with her grandson snuggled under her arm the way I used to sleep with my arm over Liam. The man across from her peeled a green apple, leveraged a slice of pale flesh between the blade and his thumb, and directed it to his mouth without taking his eyes from the fields that passed the window.

Liam's condition would have sentenced him to only be able to watch the world pass. He'd never walk, or talk, or feed himself, maybe not even think. I couldn't imagine not being able to think about what it all means. Isn't that why we are here—not to find the meaning of life, but to ask the question of each other? To know each other so we won't get lost on our way home from this circus?

People up and down the train car craned their heads out into the aisle to watch the spectacle of me, the foreign woman, climb the narrow metal ladder to the top bunk, which was a plank four feet above my head and a maximum of sixteen inches from the roof of the impenetrable, metal train car that held me captive. The rungs were so narrow that only one hiking boot would fit on a rung at a time. I tripped on my long skirt with almost every step, but I didn't want to lift it even shin-high with nearly the whole car watching me.

I thought about Liam and how he would have felt, more realistically how I would have felt, if he had grown older and people began to stare at his body that would be crumpled with disuse and be spasmodically out of his control with seizures.

As I lay in the bunk I couldn't sleep; I felt like I was in a coffin.

In the mornings I climbed down and sat motionless by the window watching the world pass. I was paralyzed with anxiety and couldn't go out to the platforms when we stopped. Chris went and returned offering me food, but I had no appetite. He attempted conversation and shared apples with the other passengers, but I couldn't bring myself to engage. At night, if I did pass away from wakefulness, I woke with fits and starts jolted by the metal box that held me. I passed almost two days in that confined space.

In those almost seven weeks of June and July I was afraid for Liam to die; I was afraid for Liam to live.

Bitter Roots and Jasmine Tea

Where are you? Some kind of intrusion factor it takes always
longing to cross a border. And who unexpectedly will loom
into the picture crossing you with their life stream. Who are
you & what do you do? And where were you & what did
you see? And what touched you? Who? What? Where are
you? The affairs of this conglomerate heart stretch the miles
it takes to conjure them up. Back, back to where you were.
There. To sing for my supper. To honor the deities of any
place, restore out of terrorism this song, and in the disguise
of this one body I will report on what touches the heart even
as it is tough with travel. Where are you? . . .
—*Anne Waldman*

W E FOUND A TAXI AT THE CHENGDU STATION without too much trouble. Even with the windows rolled up
we could smell the stale air. On almost every corner banners competed: one rallied the citizens to "Make Chengdu China's
Number One Tourist City"; another tried to convince tourists,
"Chengdu: China's Most Beautiful City." Sometimes they appealed

to both at once, "Chengdu, Number One Tourist City and Make Chengdu China's Most Beautiful." Our red taxi moved through streets narrow and teeming with more bicyclists than motorists. The dark waves of people on bikes rolled up alongside of our cab at every stop on our way to the Traffic Hotel. It was soothing to see all those wheels moving at once in the same direction. I wished for jet hair, not my own obvious straw. I wanted to put on the blue jacket and blue pants and blend in, and not be so other and isolated in the vehicle that conveyed me with its meter ticking away.

The Traffic Hotel looked expensive as we approached then stopped in front. I panicked; the cab driver must have misunderstood. I thought he'd taken us to the wrong place.

"This can't be it. Ask him if this is it." I sat up straight in the seat and looked window to window.

"It's okay, Katie. I can see the sign right there. It's right. It's okay," Chris said.

"Oh," I felt silly and tried to make my tone more appropriate as a way of saying sorry, "Boy, this is nice for a cheap hotel. I was expecting something like a dingy hostel."

We paid the driver and checked into the hotel. The room was ten yuan a night, which was a little more than a dollar. We paid for three nights. In the lobby was a dim gift shop: calligraphy and scenic scrolls, jade chops and figurines. A small area with tables and chairs was sectioned off by a railing. There was a counter to buy Fanta, Coke, stamps, postcards, Pringles, film, beer, and water. We made our way up to room 412.

Inside the room, the first thing I did was change my clothes and lose the smell of the 50-hour train ride from Guangzhou. Looking in the dresser mirror, I saw myself standing in the middle of the room naked. Chris was off to the side and not reflected in the glass. It was the first time since I left home that I'd stood bare for any length of time. It felt good to be unclothed, especially after being trapped on the train and shrouded in the same skirt, tee shirt, and sweatshirt. Across my stomach several inches below my belly button the scar of my incision was still bright red and welted. I ran my fingers over it, massaging the scar so it would heal better. I wondered how long it would be before it faded. I turned to Chris who was digging fresh socks out of his pack.

"I like my scar. And my Liam lines." I smiled at Chris and indicated the stretch marks and great scar that marked my now-hollow, deflated belly. I tried to see my ugly parts in a different way, a way like one of the *Twenty-One Praises of Tara* describes: "casting off the flaws of (my) body, she (I; Tara) possess perfect great and minor marks." I was still earning my stripes, like any other mother does once she is stretched beyond herself and begins rearing. But unlike most other mothers, I was left to justify from a razed future a reasonable understanding of why we'd suffered so much. I couldn't accept that such a profound loss was not also somehow proportionally meaningful. Instead of raising my wise-eyed baby, my only sunshine, I was trying to raise from nothing a reason that would hold up the sun for me. I was trying to not let my life set into that frightening, dark place three steps beyond devastation, into which a suddenly childless mother is delivered.

I glanced in the mirror and admired the new pendant I bought in Hong Kong for my upcoming birthday. It was a pearl and three tiny diamonds. I paid more for it then a better bargainer would have, but to me I got what I paid for and to me it was more. Liam's birthstone was a pearl. Not every oyster shell has a pearl. The Buddha, Sangha, and the Dharma are referred to as the Triple Gem. I ran the pendant across its white gold chain and thought about that simple object, and laid it down at my throat just above my heart.

...

LATER, after we settled in, we got a map from the front desk before we went for a walk to see what else we could find to touch our hearts. The map read, "Brief Introduction Of Chengdu's Famous scenic spot. Renovated Hunan River has clear water, green bank, long bridge mirrored in the river, yachts sailing on the water, just like jadite necklace inlaid with bright pearls, she's new scenic route of the city." The first thing we noticed about Hunan River, which was just one block away from the Traffic Hotel, was that it didn't flow. It moved like gray gelatin. Its banks stank like urine. Wrappers, cups, a hat, newspapers, and cans were inlaid on the surface; the water was so thickly polluted that the items neither sank nor moved out of sight as we crossed the long bridge to the tea pavilion. The river mirrored no bridge as promised, but like my mind, it held mementos of the past and was unable to move forward at a natural pace.

From the distance of the tea pavilion the river was scenic. A network of tables reached out from the tea stall toward the river. We took a seat and waited, looking around to figure out what we were supposed to do next. I noticed that a man was serving the tables, so we waited rather than approach the tea stall. It was midday and almost all of the tables were full. Most people were wearing the same simple, cloth slippers. A man read a paper, two women talked, leaning into one another, one woman fished a ringing cell phone out of her black leather purse as the waiter set a cup in front of her, then poured steaming water into it from a long cylindrical thermos.

Tea is not just tea in Asian cultures. It is an art, drinking and serving tea. For hundreds of centuries, tea ceremonies have occasioned a host and guest to sit quietly and strive for spiritual refreshment and universal harmony. Tea has steeped family occasions, weddings, and prayer sessions. Simple cups have been shared to offer respect, gratitude, apology—to beseech. Tibetan Buddhists hold pujas and offer overflowing cups of tea to the deities. Tea at Tibetan marriage engagements is essential; it represents everlasting ties. Tea inspires poetry and song, and connects people, and lets us speak to the buddhas.

We sat, at the tea pavilion, for some time before we realized we needed to somehow order tea. "I'll go find out what to do," Chris said and left me cupped in the chatter around me. The twittering of the blowing leaves overhead, and the birdsong, and the people next to me all melted indistinguishably together since to me the words were no more decodable than the conversation of the breeze and birds in the trees.

I lit a cigarette and noticed my hands were shaking slightly though I felt calmer than I had in days. I never thought I'd smoke again after giving it up when I got pregnant, and now this familiar ritual made me sad even though it settled my nerves. I negotiated with myself everyday reasons to keep going. Sometimes that contract was made with the contact in a stranger's eye, sometimes a lovely view from a cramped and speeding train, a wave rolling in from the Pacific, the comfortable silence that Chris and I kept, a secret pact. In a silent hospital hall waiting for the elevator doors to open, we had made a promise to Liam—so we wouldn't disappoint him, and each other—to not give up, to not let go of each other, so Liam's legacy would not be broken spirits, but happiness living beyond this sorrow.

Chris returned with two covered cups each containing a small gathering of pale jasmine tea leaves. The scent seeping from the tightly curled leaves waiting to be unfurled in the warm bath of the tea bowl was of green shoots, and blossoms, and serenity, and joy, and so lovely I wanted to smile and cry all at once.

"The guy with the thermos will come around in a minute," Chris said.

I cradled the cup in my hands just under my nose, drinking in the satisfying fragrance, a sacred prayer. I waited for the restorative hot water that would transform the dry leaves in my empty cup.

We sat in the park by the river for hours, looking at the people around us and mostly not talking. A younger man sat down a few tables away and was approached by a hunched old man pointing to the younger man's feet. In his wizened hand he held a pair of simple cloth slippers. They exchanged a nod, and the man traded his shoes for the slippers. As the older man walked away he had already begun to shine the younger man's shoes with a dingy rag.

Three women sat around a small table; their hands cracked peanuts and pried out the meat letting shells drop at their feet. Their words fell from their mouths quickly as more shells dropped to the hulls already mounded at their feet.

There was a ritual I couldn't quite decipher; a man with a long silver rod seemed to be shoving it in the ear of a woman whose head was cocked to one side. Chris speculated he was performing some Chinese form of curbside lobotomy.

The next table over a slender man with fingers like reeds was massaging the neck, head, and shoulders of a man whose dangling arms and drooping shoulders advertised the skill of the masseur.

The thermos man made the rounds to all those people, and us, filling our cups; when he removed the lid, the leaves danced to the top in a swirl, a reverse whirlpool, from the motion of pouring water. He replaced the lid leaving a sliver-moon of leafy tea uncovered. The jasmine rose to meet me, gently warming and slightly wetting my face like the breath of a baby.

Silver Ear-Rod Man had moved closer to us and was beginning his procedure on his next customer. He stood in back of the woman, and with a practiced twirl he swirled cotton onto the end of the silver rod, then gently tilted the woman's head to her shoulder and swabbed her ear. I was delighted by that uninhibited display of hygiene.

"Chris, you should get your ears cleaned," I said.

"I don't think so."

I did talk him into a shoulder massage and then haggled about the price for him: forty yuan.

I paid about the same for a bamboo flute from a man who strolled by playing one from his shoulder bag. The flute man showed me how to hold the flute to get a note. He played, and I tried to imitate him for some time, which I did quickly at first but couldn't do consistently. I started to hand the flute back to the man indicating I didn't want to buy it.

"What? You can't not buy it now," Chris insisted. "You made him stand there for about half an hour showing you how to play it."

"So?" I said. But I did feel guilty and bargained for the flute.

"I can't believe you paid forty yuan for that." Chris laughed at me.

"What, Chris? You said to buy it, and then you make fun of me?" I waved him away with my flute. "Whatever," I said to emphasize my light-hearted dismissal as I brought the flute to my mouth.

We dubbed it "the five-dollar bamboo stick," since I was unable to get another note from it.

The flute man walked away trilling notes full and ripe like small plums as he went.

On November 8, I turned twenty-eight, but I felt eighty-two. For my birthday I wouldn't be having a party. No cake. No wishes; there was no use in that. I felt old and used up. Spent. I felt distant from everything, like I'd died already.

As I dressed that day I said to Chris, "I'm gonna try to have a good day today."

He gave me a yellow rose he had snuck away to find. We decided to spend the day walking and just see what we found. We headed across the Long Bridge. Just on the other side of it, in a clearing before the park began, a group of people were doing tai chi. I followed along for a few poses. I missed the practice I had given up a short time ago and was pleased to know my body had not yet forgotten that meditative martial dance.

We walked by the tea pavilion. The shelters were not yet open. The chairs were empty. We walked along the bank of the river. An old man came up the embankment, relieved, zipping up his pants as he crossed our path. In another clearing, at the end of the park, a record played and couples waltzed. They didn't look down or at each other. It was like they were dancing with the music alone, and their partner was just a mirror image of themselves.

At the corner an old woman wearing a necklace of bear teeth had laid out her wares on a blanket: bundles of herbs, a bear's claw, star anise, antlers, seahorses—I would almost swear there was the horn of a unicorn though I'm sure now it was some other, more basic appendage. We walked following the crowd.

On another bridge a woman stood perfectly still with her head bowed, the point of her straw hat jutted out at the crowd like punctuation. She was silent and faceless and held a large sign tied around her neck with a rope no thicker than a noodle. I couldn't read the characters, but her bowed head made me think of shame. The other people in the street did not pay any attention to her sign.

We wandered down a narrow street and turned a corner into an outdoor food market. There were full tables: leafy greens, maybe bok choy, maybe mustard greens; melons, in all sizes and shapes, some green, some pale orange; chickens live and clucking in cages, some dead and bare of their feathers hanging from their feet on a rope strung across the stall; green beans, casks of bean curd; small round burlap sacks open on a table with their moons of rice glowing from inside—the bags of brown and wild rice looked like eclipses.

A long time ago, growing up exposed to another doctrine, I heard, "If you have faith the size of a mustard seed nothing will be impossible for you." That's a truth that I can accept still. What did I see in front of me now that I was positioned firmly on the path that will guide my future, even in a country that forbade the practice of any kind of faith? I saw simple salt-of-the-earth things: bitter but fortifying mustard greens grown from the tiniest seeds, an open-air market with choices to make, and a sea of people in uniform clothing that was unfamiliar to me and whose carriage and physical characteristic I was unaccustomed to seeing; all of these images and thoughts that I took in allowed me to really see others in a different way, and it was suddenly clear—overwhelming and at the same time a relief to know—the truth of the matter is that we're all not so impossibly different.

At a fish stall, a man beheaded a large fish on a wooden table blackened with age and the years of guts, and scales, and blood that had spilled over it. It looked smooth like lacquer. Just next to him a small boy stood behind a crate—a chopping block of his own playful design. On it was a fish head that he chopped at with a stick.

It was the radishes at the next stall that caught my eye. They were red with green leaves lacy from insect bites in the field and large as potatoes. I decided to make a meal of this sharp root that grows best when the earth is cold. I tried to buy one from the plump vendor, but she wouldn't take my money. She gave me the bitter root and shooed me away with a smile. The pungent flesh tasted like water and dirt all at the same time. It was elemental, that bitter and bright tuber; it, with the woman's smile, satisfied me for a while.

Soon, we realized we'd lost our way.

"Where are we? Where are we?" I started to cry.

Chris got out the map to reorient us, but I had to keep moving.

Chris ran to catch up to me, "Where are you going?"

"Nowhere," I yelled. Tears were streaming down my face by then. "I'm nowhere and it's my birthday. I have nothing, no job, no baby, and no idea where we are. I don't know who I am."

"Katie, it's okay." He tried again to calm me but his voice sounded scared, and that scared me and made me feel more out of control. "Where do you want to go? What do you want?" He continued.

"I want Liam back!" I came undone with tears not caring who saw me. I stood in the middle of the sidewalk, but I felt like I was looking down on myself—a speck in a dark and foreign place. "I don't know where to go. I don't want to be here, or home, or anywhere." At that moment time and space imploded and was all nothing. We are all nothing. We are all empty shells—fish heads disembodied, cups waiting to be filled, yellow roses, promises, bitter roots, coded conversations, spinning wheels, parents' children, a prayer, rituals to decipher, a dance, notes like ripe plums, pushing hands, a bridge above a river, steam above a cup. Life is a stream rushing by. We get born fast and we move along like burning stars. All we can do is remember the conglomerate sights that unexpectedly touched our rough, travel-worn hearts, hoping it will trace back to where we are, hoping faith enough to move us along remains.

We both knew there were no words to comfort either one of us, so we walked and I continued to cry with no regard, until no more tears came. I wanted to keep walking until there were no more days.

The slicing sun pressed down on me. The tomb-like darkness of the teahouses that lined the street was inviting.

"Wanna get tea?" I asked calmly as the emotional squall had

washed over me and taken the fearful fight out of me, for now. I'd come back to myself somewhat subdued, my emotions and nerves receded beneath my placid, for now, surface. "Sorry about before," I added.

"Yeah, let's get some tea." He nodded toward the darkened door of a teahouse two steps ahead.

I WAS BLINDED, momentarily, by the dark, cool interior as I stepped out of the bright afternoon and into the teahouse. It was narrow with a low ceiling. There were only a few teak tables and chairs all pressed in close. Light, steam, and smoke from the large kettle on a semi-open fire in the back filled the small space. When I sat I realized how swollen my feet were, how achy my legs were, how tired I was. There was one old man at a corner table next to a thick bamboo ladder that went nowhere. His beard was long and wispy; his eyes were rheumy coal and betrayed nothing of what he thought of our presence. The wizened man and I regarded each other as benign spectators just passing through. I didn't feel unwelcome or invited and that felt comfortable to me.

"*Ni-hao,*" Chris said when the proprietress came to our table. "Hello" was one of the only words we mastered, but it seemed to go a long way if you sang it out with a smile. Chris ordered our tea in pantomime. When it was served, in a white porcelain cup with blue flowers stark against the blood-red lacquer of the table top, I felt like a little bit of comfort had been placed within my reach. "*Shey-shey,*" I thanked her as she tipped the lid to the side releasing the steam and aroma—an essential, earthy smell of jasmine, dirt, and vetiver. I let the leaves steep in my birthday tea, said a blessing, cleared the steam with the palm of my hand, and took the liquid prayer to my lips.

The tea was strong like I wanted to be.

Stand Sorrowing and Delighted in Sacred Rain

They say there is beauty in this sadness, it's true, a change will come, a change will come to you. You've got your own way of lookin' at life and its perils, got your own way of feelin' its pain, you've got your way of dealing with the trouble in mind, got your own way of knowin' how to stand in the rain. Go on and stand in the rain.

—Elana Arian

URNING THE CORNER FROM HOYT STREET into the hospital driveway, the rain fell and I believe it was unusually cold for summer in Oregon. We were going for a routine weekly check-up with my midwife. At the red light just before we turned, the rain beat into a puddle in the middle of the street. The light changed. The car turned. Chris was driving. I turned my head back to that portent puddling-up, unable to take my eyes from it. Maybe I sensed something? Perhaps I wanted to stay in that moment before the turn for the worse when just the rain was falling, before the ultrasound in the midwife's office had registered a faint irregularity of heartbeat a week before my due date, before Liam got born so fast, before we learned that he wouldn't live long, burning like a shooting star through those cool mid-summer days.

It was the beginning of the Something Worse summer. Every new bit of information about our baby's condition we learned seemed awful, like the worst news we could get—and then we learned worse news still. I had to learn things, that summer, I never wanted to know in order to take care of Liam. I also learned things I needed to know, and learned that, as awful as things got, I wasn't immune to a pleasant surprise.

To feed him I learned to insert a nasogastric feeding tube into his nose. I measured it from his cheek to his stomach along his seized-up body and pinched the tube at the point where it touched just below his nose. I fumbled with one hand to plug my ears with the miniature stethoscope—the one the nurse at the NICU gave me when we decided to take our baby home—so I could listen. I didn't let go of the tube. I didn't want to lose the length I'd measured off. I flipped the tube over and began inserting it into Liam's nose and noticed that his nose looked like his father's and that his eyes were sometimes the color of sapphires. Perhaps, if things were right, they'd be blue someday. But nothing was right, there wouldn't be a someday—only that minute and my son's unblinking stare.

I learned to move slowly, to bend with the pressure.

I slowly pushed the small plastic tube into Liam's nose, feeling it hit the back of his nasal cavity. With the tiniest amount of pressure it bent and continued down his throat. I continued feeding the tube into his nose until my fingers, pinched around the tube, were just under his nostril. Then came the important part. I had to listen to what was inside his body. I connected a large nutritional syringe, the kind that has no needle, to the end of the tube. I unwrapped

Liam from the blankets and exposed his tummy. I pressed the pad of the stethoscope to his tummy just above his navel, and got ready to listen.

I waited for the cars passing and the dogs barking outside to stop, then pushed the plunger on the syringe forcing a bit of air down the tube. I had to make sure I heard a little squeak through the stethoscope. Then I'd know that the tube was in the right place, in his stomach and not in his esophagus or windpipe. I pressed the plunger a couple of cc further, and then listened for a couple of more cc if I didn't hear it.

The tiniest, almost imperceptible, noise was my assurance that he wouldn't drown in mother's milk. He could've choked. He could have died right then while I was trying to feed him, if I made a mistake. I had to make sure I heard it right. I had to back the plunger up and listen again until I did. But I couldn't do it more than a couple of times because if I filled his stomach with air there wouldn't be room for milk, and then he'd have to wait to eat—though he wouldn't cry; he never really did. I only had a couple of shots to get it right, so I listened. I did as best as I could to listen to what was inside of him, and get it right, for his sake. I learned that abnormal could feel normal since I'd never known "normal."

Once I knew the tube was placed correctly, I drew 43 cc of milk into the syringe. The doctors said formula was okay. But I pumped and gave him breast milk instead. He may have had an inadequate sucking reflex and an inefficient draw, making him unable to nurse, but at least I could give him that. "Liquid gold," my favorite NICU nurse called it. I attached the end of the syringe to the end of the feeding tube. The inattentive nurse on the night shift—not the favorite one who kept me sane and called the two-foot-by-three-foot Plexiglass box with lights and wires and warmers that held Liam "sacred ground," the other one whose pronunciation I had to correct every time she said Liam's name—she hammered down the plunger, forcing all the milk in at one blast, expanding his stomach with a quick rush of milk; three seconds and the meal was over and she'd rush out the door of the private room in the NICU they let us sleep in with Liam while we watched over him.

I couldn't feed him like that. It made my milk seem like prescription drugs, a perfunctory chore, rather than the sweet nourishment and the normal ritual it should have been. At home, I propped Liam on my bent legs, leaned back against the hard wall, and made myself cozy on the bed. I raised the syringe above my head with my hand so the milk flowed slowly and gently into Liam's stomach. It took time for all the milk to drain. I was happy to pretend I had all the time in the world. In the meantime, I rocked Liam back and forth on my knees and sang, "You are my sunshine, my only sunshine. You make me happy when skies are gray."

I tried not to think about the copy of the Do Not Resuscitate order that was on the coffee table on the other side of the wall in the living room. "You'll never know, dear, how much I love you. Please don't take my sunshine away."

I tried not to think about what would come next. I had no idea what and when any change would come anyway. He couldn't use an NG tube forever. The next intervention after that would be a direct gastric tube. They would have to cut his stomach and place a plastic tube in with a capped-off end that would stick out like a tire airplug. I kept singing, "The other night, dear, as I lay sleeping, I dreamed I held you in my arms." It may not come to that, the doctors said. But if it didn't, it meant that it had come to something even worse. "When I awoke, dear, I was not with you, and I hung my head and cried."

I learned I had to hold on any way I could, even knowing the end would come soon.

After some time the last of the milk passed through the syringe into the tube. I watched the white line of the milk drain down. My arm got tired but I held on anyway supporting my raised elbow with my other hand when I needed to. The line slipped into his nose; the tube was cleared. I waited a couple of heartbeats more, a verse more, to make sure the milk had passed all the way into his stomach. I removed the syringe, taped off the tube, and taped it to his cheek for the next feeding. I didn't need to change it until the next day. I hoped I'd have to change it the next day because if I didn't, it meant something even worse had happened; I'd have to do something even worse. Learn to let go.

I learned I had to make decisions I didn't want to make. My father-in-law, Jerry, arrived after flying for three days from St. Petersburg, Russia, to be with us. Chris had sent a fax to his boat, "Come now, please." Jerry was a cardiac-thoracic surgeon and head of surgery for Maine Medical Hospital, but in his transition to retirement he took a job as a doctor on a Maine Maritime Academy ship sailing to Russia from Maine. He told us about a nurse onboard who had a niece or nephew who was born Very Sick too. ("Very Sick" was hospital code for babies who were likely to die. I, unfortunately, learned that and lots of other jargon I'd rather be ignorant of: severe hypoxic ischemic encephalopathy and aortic thrombus.) That baby that the nurse told him about had an NG tube too, for a while.

"You can make a choice," Jerry said as we sat in my living room where the late-afternoon sun had begun to fill the room with warmth, and the butter-yellow walls began to glow. "People do make that decision in some extreme cases."

I took in his words, but couldn't comment on them directly. "I love this glowy time of day." I said looking down on Liam in my arms. "It's so bright and soft. I like to think of it as a golden hour."

Jerry, I think, sort of chortled and looked down. In my stupid arrogance, I thought he just liked my phrase and was pondering it. Maybe he did tell me "the golden hour" is also medical slang. But I don't think he explained it to me then. It was years later I learned that in the ER medical community "the golden hour" is the period of time from the onset of the injury, that if the right remedy is applied, then the patient is likely to be saved. The physicians had just a short time, only a few chances to get it right.

I could only sit in the afternoon light holding my bright little baby and listen.

WHEN JERRY WAS GETTING READY TO LEAVE a few days later I was in the other room changing Liam's diaper. I hurried and brought him out and asked Jerry if he wanted to hold Liam one last time before he left. He took Liam in his arms and cried. I'd never seen Jerry cry. When he was at his car door he turned back and said, through the wide-open space between us all, "I love you."

The decisions we had to make didn't seem like decisions; they seemed like sentences.

We had decided to sign the Do Not Resuscitate papers a week after we brought Liam home. Chris and Liam and I sat with our hospice nurse in silence for a long time when I laid the paper down on the table after signing it. What else could we do? Hearts breaking are oppressively silent.

The end of Liam's life could come in five days, five minutes, five seconds, without warning. Another week after we signed the DNR papers we decided to discontinue the NG tube and the seizure medication, which were the only interventions we didn't discontinue when we left the hospital. The doctors said he probably wouldn't live long enough for us to have to make that decision. Discontinuing the feeding tube felt like the most horrible thing we could do.

It was hard to imagine, it still is, that the worst thing we could think of was actually the best thing we could do to help Liam. It was an astonishing occurrence, an anguishing blessing, that Liam lived for almost four more weeks without a feeding tube, unable to nurse, and without medication. It was something that a neonatal nurse with thirty years experience had never seen happen for a baby who was so Very Sick.

I FELT LITERALLY SHATTERED. Knowing our son could die at any moment, there was an actual physical feeling that all the cells of my body were exploding and flying out from me. Every face and flower and song had more than one meaning; the universe was telling me a story, life had a narrative of its own. Every dream told me a new secret, and I was trying to take it all in to make sense of this catastrophe so utterly awful it was absurd. That obsession with interpreting the signs around me transformed everything I saw from then on; it still does. I guess I was desperate to find meaning and reason in that unreasonable situation; I sought it out and saw meaning and symbolism everywhere, obsessively.

Ordinary things in an average day that summer were different too.

I learned to make do.

I had to make sure I had a blanket with me when I went to the grocery store not just to keep Liam warm, but because I might need it to cover him up if he died while I was in the store.

I wanted people we knew to meet him, but made sure the visits were short. Only a few of our closest friends came to our house for longer than a half-hour. When other people were around, I became more aware of how different Liam's behavior was from a healthy baby's and it hurt too much to be aware of that for too long, and for anyone else to see it.

The cards and flowers that arrived when we got home from the hospital said "thinking of you" and offered condolences instead of congratulations for the birth of our son.

Near the end, he'd grown so thin strangers were surprised when I told them how old he was. Sometimes I lied and said yes, he was born premature. Sometimes I didn't have the strength to lie, told them the truth, and felt bad for them when the shock of it registered on their faces.

I learned ordinary days and average things were all impermanent illusions too.

Living a life, I learned, while waiting for death was like living in the space where one breath ends and the other has not yet begun; it was like sleepwalking through my worst nightmare feeling more awake, and acutely aware, than I ever had been in my life; it was like drowning in thin air; like standing on a deserted shore in awe of a squall that was pulling back and gathering its force to crush me. I learned I could be, at the same time, overwhelmed with natural great love for my child who was teaching me more than I could have learned in thirty-three lifetimes without him, even though the one I gave him was rushing by quicker than most.

Liam had an equanimous presence, and was astonishingly beautiful, like a Tibetan blue poppy, a sublime and rare blossom, once thought to be mythical. I am told still by the handful of people who met him that he compelled them to think in a way they never had, and that he still comes to mind even though it was a short time he was here and it's been a long time he's been gone.

The poppy's petals, an uncommon blue, evoke with its hue the cloudless sky, the vast ocean, or the true nature of the mind that abides in equanimity despite unrelenting waves of illusion and always-changing clouds of desire and attachment. In the center of the poppy's cupped-petals are mustard-yellow stamens—a bright, happy contrast to the profound, solemn blue that surrounds them. In the center of that Something Worse summer there was, despite it all, Liam. And there were some things to learn. It's natural that two aspects of one thing so different in shading, like joy and sorrow, exist side-by-side, one within the other. And the blue poppy's beauty is undiminished by the true, sad fact that it won't last forever, maybe not very long at all.

When Liam died I tried to hold on to that new appreciation for accepting all aspects, the light and dark, of any situation, allowing for the joy that was the gift of his presence to take root in my life, instead of the pain and anger that his loss left. To bloom in mid-July, blue poppies require cool temperatures; they need the cold if they're going to flourish. That summer brought a cold reality of existence to life for me; I had to accept the hardship and pain with the beauty and happiness.

To see a gift amid my devastation could not have been a harder thing for me to do. But I wanted to believe it wasn't impossible. I hoped it wasn't an anathema to embrace that gift, as repugnant as it may at first seem to others to see my devastation as a teaching, a source from which to grow, and a chance to change my mind about what it means to be blessed with a rare human birth. A changed mind came to me for having known Liam. The less-awake person I was before passed away. I learned I knew how to stand—grateful—in the rain when he was with me, when I was filled up with sorrow and delight.

Artful Moments of Ordinary Days

An artist wears her art in place of wounds.
—*Patti Smith*

W HILE WE WAITED FOR LIAM TO DIE we tried to not stop living, and like any new mommy, I wanted to capture those moments and hold on to them—those elusive points of light that come together in the camera, captured to develop after the moment has been lost. Life is fleeting; the bulb flashes, the shutter blinks, and I'm comforted to know the impression will be with me. I can then let go a bit, appreciate the artful moments of ordinary days, and enjoy them flashing by.

We all want those keepsake moments of life, and we want happiness, and not to suffer. We want the spacious, at-ease frame of mind that comes when we trust that two opposing thoughts can both be true. Someone can be present with me and not here at all. Having nothing can be the same as having it all. Milarepa, the poet-saint of Tibet, wrote in *Drinking the Mountain Stream* that "happy is one who knows Samsara and Nirvana are not two."

As if looking through a viewfinder of a camera, I looked at life differently now. Details were singled out, and signaled out. I looked for the narrative in the street scene, in my life, I looked into life rather than at it. I looked at the relief on the door rather than the house, the smile on the baby's face in the pram rather than the mother walking by. The camera shielded me and at the same time allowed me to feel drawn in closer. I took around 390 pictures of Liam and our too-few adventures and ordinary moments together.

The shutter blinked: We picnicked at Mount Tabor Park, which is the only active volcano inside a city's limits. From there we had a view of Mount Hood in the distance. It was a rare clear day. We stretched out in the grass of one unexploded mountain, and ate grapes, and cheese, and rustic bread, and sipped a beer looking into the distance at another unexploded mountain. For that day we were just a family on a picnic in the sunshine.

A HIGH LAMA, Her Eminence Jetsun Chimey Luding, sometimes called Jetsun Kusho, came to town for a two-day teaching. I had had a student/teacher relationship with her since I was seventeen when I attended my first Buddhist teaching. I can't discern if it was the Mahakala or Mahakali empowerment she gave—but either way the merit gained is similar; they are the male and female aspects of the same deity who is a fierce protector of the dharma and of practitioners on the path.

I really wanted Jetsun-la to give Liam a blessing so we brought him to her teachings on compassion. I don't recall the exact words of the teaching, but I do remember a flash of realization as I sat on the cushion rocking Liam in his car seat. No matter if people felt we made the right or wrong decisions for Liam, I was ready to accept the responsibility. I was his mother and it was my job to protect him no matter what. His father and I did what no one else could or would do. We thought it best at the time of his birth to intervene and deliver him by C-section and resuscitate him. We decided to intervene and give him drugs to keep his heart beating in those dire first few days, and drugs to prevent seizures, and tubes to take in food.

And then we decided further intervention was denying him the opportunity to move past this suffering. We decided to protect him from suffering rather than death.

After the teaching, on the second day, we took Liam to the front of the room where Jetsun-la was sitting. We brought a *kata*, a white scarf, which we'd offer and she'd return draped over his neck for a blessing. We also asked her to give Liam a Tibetan Dharma name. She gave him her own father's name. She called him Kunga Namgyal—"Happiness or Joy Victorious." I hoped that she was right. I hope for Liam, and for us.

I told her about the many dreams I had of Buddhist lamas when I was pregnant with Liam and asked her what they could mean. She seemed a bit surprised and said it sounded like he was a *tulku*, a reincarnated lama, but that he had just a few obstacles of past karma that he needed to overcome in this life. After most of the people had left, Jetsun-la called us to her side again. She wanted to hold Liam and give him a special blessing. She took him, wrapped in his rainbow-silk and flannel blanket, in her arms. She put her forehead to his, which is a sign of respect for Tibetans; it says, "Your mind is like my mind. The same mind." She blessed him again. She gave us a pinch of blessed powder to feed to him and said it would bring him clarity.

I have a picture of my own tulku taken as my lama held him on that day, which is sitting on my altar where I make offerings for the blessings of my past, and where I try meditate—to sight my future—by cultivating a good frame of mind.

...

SHUTTER BLINKED: We took him to the forest at Opal Creek and walked with him through the old growth. I walked slowly up the dirt and strewn-leaves incline, because in my second post-operative week, every step pierced me. Chris and I took turns carrying him and watching him watch the wide canopy overhead, a kaleidoscope of light and leaves that shimmered and hushed with the breeze. We rested in the low branching elbows of trees along the trail. I made a miniature wildflower bouquet. We paused at a rushing fall. We were a family hiking in an oasis; for the day, nothing more.

AFTER LIAM PASSED AWAY we went to a Tara meditation retreat with Jetsun-la in the San Juan Islands of Washington State. When I met with her alone one afternoon, I cried and told her I was too sad to meditate and do the practice, which was a prescribed set of visualizations and mantras. She said I should do it anyway. I should do the Vajrasattva practice, a purification ritual, for Liam. I told her I felt bad about the decisions not to pursue further medical interventions that may have prolonged his life. She asked me what the doctors told us to do. She said if we did what they thought we should do then I shouldn't feel bad. The problem was that the doctors never told us what to do. They gave us a diagnosis, probable outcomes, and decisions to make.

Of course I would make any trade to give him a healthy life, but that wasn't an option. Someone would say forgoing surgeries, and medications, and therapies, and a stomach-tube to help him live longer was horrible, and I would agree. I wanted to do all that but it wasn't going to help Liam walk, or laugh, or nurse, or think. It would only have made us feel better. I didn't want to suffer, but I wanted more for Liam not to suffer. It was a hopeless situation. The only hope was letting go, believing that his next life would be better, knowing the rest of my life would be painfully absent of him, and painfully full of anguishing doubts about those decisions. Liam was going to die no matter what we did or didn't do. But, what we did or didn't do would affect how much he suffered. We had to stop trying to be in control and let his karma, and ours, be the guide. Mind leads the way, but our actions chart the course.

SHUTTER BLINKED: We took Liam to Cannon Beach and walked against gently blowing sand, watching the waves crash against Haystack Rock. Our lifetimes keep rolling in and crashing on this shore of existence. The sky and the Willamette River running to the cold Pacific were shades of blue like the colors that swirl in the petals of blue poppies, coming together to make an astonishing result. Liam did crinkle his face a bit when the wind and sand blew at him; I was delighted that he noticed his surroundings at all and made a nest for him in my lap to shield him. There were clouds, but they were unpunishing puffs and drifting. In the pictures we took, and for that day, Liam was in our arms with our backs to the sea and we were smiling.

BLINK: On Father's Day we thought we should go out. We went to Il Piato, which was a little elegantly appointed but comfortable neighborhood place offering perfect saltimbocca, pastas al dente with full sauces, and complex wines to complement. It traditionally had been our celebrating place. We'd decadently indulge. But that night I ordered something more comforting, risotto with smoked cheese and colorful vegetables. I gave Chris his first and, for the foreseeable future, only Father's Day present. It was a slender silver cuff bracelet with simple stars stamped into it. But that night I could take in none of the goodness. The smoke of my dish was so over-powering I thought I might vomit. I actually kept looking over my shoulder to see if the kitchen was on fire; something really had to be burning down for the wood taste to sit so heavy on my tongue.

Mid-meal Chris asked if I wanted to go, sensing my spark of

anguish. I looked around the table at the three of us. Liam was in his car seat on the chair between us. I nodded, "Yes, we have to go home. I can't do this." I couldn't choke down any more tears. I thought I would explode in an embarrassing torrent of tears even before the bill came. Chris paid. I carried Liam in his seat out to the car and got in the back seat with him. Between sobs I apologized to Chris for ruining his Father's Day.

BLINK: Bath-time, a ritual. I avoided giving Liam a bath every day like our hospice nurse had suggested when I told her I felt awful not being able to do something more. I told myself I didn't want him to get colder, or to get a cold, to get sicker and die sooner. But honestly there was a deeper-sunk fear and truth. I panicked a little bit in those warm baths where I held him floating between my legs. The way he stretched and arched his back toward the water, sinking his head down to the rims of his eyes, and maybe beyond if I'd have let him, his arms and legs unfurled, a precious reprieve, like tea leaves in a cup.

I projected that he must think he's back in the womb. All the warm water must remind him of a safe place. He sighed when the water enveloped him. He seemed to enjoy it. We said, "He loved it." Perhaps it is me who loved to think he could recognize the warm safety of pre-birth days when everything was right and ok, or even recognize his current surroundings. I washed the warm water over him, and over me, but soon I was alert to the exposed parts of my body—what was submerged and what was not—and attuned to where the water's wake-line sliced along my thigh, rendering an insubstantial boundary line separating warmth and cold, water and air. Life.

BLINK: Death. Ordinary days. Samsara and Nirvana are not two.

Through the Eyes of a Howling Dark Dakini Vulture

The voyage of discovery is not in seeking
new landscapes but in having new eyes.
—*Marcel Proust*

ROM CHENGDU WE WOULD HAVE TO TAKE A TRAIN
to Xian, spend a day, visit the bird market and the famous
terra cotta clay soldiers. From Xian it would be another day
train ride to Xinning. From there the only option was a local bus that
would take three or four days. The overland route sounded like nothing but hardship from all six of the people whom we met who had
made the trip themselves. One traveler said that he got into a screaming match with a bus driver twelve hours into the ride, because the
driver wouldn't stop to let him take a pee. Once we got to Tibet there
was no guarantee the border guards would let us in. All the seasoned
travelers we spoke with said it was the worst bus ride of their lives.

Still, it wasn't until we had our packs on our backs, tickets in
hand, and had walked two blocks from the hotel to the train station

that I stopped walking and looked at Chris, and that we opted, simultaneously, off the hard road for now. He instantly read my mind and said, "Fuck this." He broke a smile for the first time in days. Quickly, he was headed back from where we came, waving over his shoulder for me to follow.

"Yeah, fuck this. What the hell are we doing?"

All the way back to the hotel and up to our new room, once we rechecked in, we laughed, rehashing our sudden decision against everything else.

I'd had my fill of hard roads for the time being. It was possible to take the easy road if we wanted. We wouldn't have to weigh the pros and cons, choose between bad and worse, or convene an ethics committee meeting to review our decision like we did with hospital officials and physicians.

"Right, it's not a test," I said.

"I don't even care about the soldiers. It was just a way to break up the trip," Chris confessed.

"It really won't cost all that much more to fly when you add up all the lodging and food for the next few days," I reasoned.

"Plus fees!"

"Plus who knows if we'd ever make it. The Chinese might send us back once we got to the border and then we'd really be fucked."

We flopped on the bed. Relieved, I was overcome by sleep more easily than I had been in quite a while. When we woke, we went to one of the several small travel agencies on the hotel property and booked our "Tour of Lhasa," the capital of Tibet. We were only able to buy air tickets if we bought the whole package that they offered.

ON THE PLANE I let Chris sit by the window so he could see the view of the Himalayas and Tibet as we approached, since I'd enjoyed that view once before when I traveled to Tibet as a student.

When we collected our bags, the sun glinted like a white diamond. Boarding the bus, the air was thin and crisp. It smelled clean, like nothing at all. I was grateful to be back in Tibet. Many Tibetans I knew could only dream of stepping on that sacred ground at the top of the world, and I was there again.

We got off the bus at the Tashi Mandala Guest House just off the main square in Lhasa. The square, in front of the Jokang temple, is one of the most sacred spots in the entire world for Tibetans and Tibetan Buddhists because it houses the most sacred relics and statues. People journeyed there from their homes miles and miles away prostrating—like the old woman on the balcony in Hong Kong—to that very spot. Though I'd not literally prostrated all the way from my home in Oregon to Tibet something inside had given way—like a body in full prostration—with every step of that journey.

It was my grief that pulled me down, and my belief in Buddhism that pushed me back up again to look for the path that would release me from this suffering. Or was it the other way around? Was it my belief in Buddhism that pulled me, compelling me to lay my grief down; and attachment to my grief that pushed me up again, struggling to find footing on this path? With every step it was a battle between attachment and letting go.

I might have let go of my grief easier if, at the time, I could have recalled Sogyal Rinpoche's differentiation between *having* something and *being attached* to it. If you held a coin on your palm turned up to the sky you *had* it; it was resting gently without your attachment. If you clenched your fist over the coin and turned your hand upside down you also had it, but now you were attached to it. Grasping. It took your energy, and focus, and attention to hold on. You were limited in what else you could pick up. Grief could be like a closed fist around treasured memories. It was consuming and a constant strain on my heart and mind. It limited the amount of happiness I was able to take in. There was little room to feel anything else in those dark, fisted days of my journey, but I tried.

WE CHECKED INTO THE TASHI MANDALA GUEST HOUSE, which roughly translates to Fortunate Universe Guest House. I didn't know it then, but it was the last we would see of our so-called tour guide. Though the agent wasn't specific, I did think that the tour would consist of more than a bus-ride to the hotel. In any case, it was okay with me. I felt more like we were pilgrims searching rather than tourists sightseeing. It suited me fine to make our way every day, unscheduled, trying to open ourselves to the world again. I set my backpack on the bed in room 312 and turned to take in the view.

I could see the Potala Palace. There was still a layer of glass and miles between the Dalai Lama's former palace and me, but at least I could see it from there. I thought about how many fathoms of sadness I had to go, but at least I could feel a little hope. The view was auspicious.

Tibetan Buddhists talk about cultivating the right view of the world as a way to alleviate suffering. I reminded myself to always remember to look out the window for another view when I was in a room, especially if that room was my mind. I sat and took in the view for some time before we decided to head out into the land of the snow lion and find something to eat. In a few days' time, our families in America would celebrate Thanksgiving. There, at the roof of the world, where we had come to view our experience, I tried to cultivate a sense of thanks for the time we did have with Liam and for what I was learning. My celebration and thanksgiving would be in my footsteps, each one that I was able to take on the path both beneath my feet and in my mind.

...

WE FOUND OUR WAY through the cold, bright Tibetan streets to a traditional *sa-kung*, a restaurant. The one we chose was up a narrow flight of stairs in a square whitewashed building. There were just a few tables in the close dark-wood beamed room. We kept our coats on because the room was almost empty, and in general the restaurants were not warmed except by the company of others. The menu was simple. *Mho-mho*s (dumplings) and *thunk-pa* (soup), with *sha* (meat) or without, was the standard.

I recalled a dream from when I was pregnant with Liam. I was in a football stadium filled with people waiting to hear a teaching by His Holiness the Dalai Lama. No one but me seemed to notice the Dalai Lama was sitting on a high bleacher step. He told me to sit down on his right. He whispered something in my ear and my head felt full of light like I'd realized something but I never heard the words. He handed me a cup of warm, salty Tibetan tea and told me to drink it. In my waking life I had tasted the traditional tea many times, but I never acquired a taste for it. In my dream I tasted it with all my senses; it was gorgeous. Nothing had ever tasted so good or soothing.

In the sa-kung, in the land from which His Holiness came but to which he could never return, I ordered the *pu-cha* (Tibetan tea) rather than the *nargmo-cha* (sweet tea) that, like most tourists, I had opted for in the past. I wanted to test my dream against reality. When the tea was served in a stout porcelain bowl, I removed the lid and the steam rose to the roof like the smoke from a butter lamp that carries a prayer to the deities. The tea, salty and oily from yak butter, was as good as in my dream. It quenched. At that moment I was awake to the elliptical nature between the world around me and the dream world beyond me. As I sat drinking tea and waiting for the *sha mho-mhos* I ordered, I remembered the other auspicious dreams that I had had when I was pregnant.

In one, I was camping in a gymnasium full of people. I lay on my cot and looked up. There was no ceiling, just the open star-filled sky. I floated up into the Himalayas. Looking to my left, I saw through the wall of a house. The Dalai Lama was sitting down to a meal with other high lamas that I couldn't name except for His Holiness Sakya Trizin and his sister, my lama, Her Eminence Jetsun Kusho. His Holiness the Dalai Lama motioned for me to sit at his side and for me to eat from the slices of meat heaped on his plate. I hesitated because it didn't seem respectful to take His Holiness's food, but he offered so I felt like I couldn't refuse. There was a full moon illuminating snow on the mountains washing them in a blushing pink and white glow.

In another dream, I climbed a twisted set of stairs to a monastery entry. There was a red curtain, and I knew the Dalai Lama was behind it. I sat down in the large shrine room reading a Tibetan text. It had the eight auspicious symbols of Buddhism on it: a conch shell, an umbrella, a victory banner, two fish touching, the endless knot, a lotus, the Dharma wheel, and a treasure vase. I think I remembered focusing on the vase. Just then the Dalai Lama walked toward me from behind the curtain. He pointed at the text, and the vase depicted in it, and said close to my ear, "That is your mind." The vase, it's taught, is your perception of existence. It's an impermanent object that separates the space inside of the vase (your mind) from the space outside of the vase (everything; emptiness). When perception is shattered, there is nothing that separates your mind from emptiness, everything that is inside of you from everything that is outside of you.

THE NEXT DAY we walked around Lhasa. The streets that were wide dirt paths when I visited many years before as a student were now paved, gray corridors of open commerce. Small, whitewashed mortar and wood structures that once held family-owned shops and restaurants with living-spaces on top floors were replaced with typical Chinese-designed cinderblock buildings crammed brick-face to brick-face. The shopkeepers looked mostly Chinese. There were now crossing signals blinking on the streets, which had been thoroughfares to carts and horses instead of smog-belching cars and scooters. Change, which had been the preoccupation of my life and thoughts, had overrun Tibet too. I don't think I thought at the time that Tibet would be exempt from the laws of impermanence, but the flashing, crowded streets of a once-serene Lhasa were a portent that weighed me down. With every step I was fighting the urge to just lie down and give up. No matter where I went, even if I ran away to the top of the world, I could not avoid the true nature of life.

As I crossed a street and stepped onto the curb, my breath stopped short and tears flooded my eyes. On the curb sat a woman in a long, matted yak-skin coat with her hand out to me. Her face was like worn leather, shiny with dirt and, probably, the yak butter that Tibetans used to protect their skin from the weather. Her black hair was braided to her waist in the traditional thin braids of the Kham region, 108 of them, symbolically representing the defilements that must be overcome to attain enlightenment. Tucked in her coat and peeking out from his repose next to his mother's bare breast was an infant. Despite his newness, he had skin as weathered as his mother's. He reached out to me, too, with his tiny new hand. He had his mother's dark imploring eyes that reached even further than his outstretched hand into my heart. I took a few more steps and tried to catch my breath to stop the tears. I turned to go back to them, but didn't know how I could help. No money I could give them would ever really be enough. It wouldn't be the solution to the real problem, the problem being that in life there is suffering, no matter who you are and where you go. I turned back to the path in front of me and willed myself to move on through the swell of confused emotions that overtook me.

Later we were in a cyber café on a rooftop near the Jokang, which was yet another reminder of how this once ancient city had been invaded by powerful forces. Another tourist caught my eyes as she passed the table where Chris and I sat. She said something like "Isn't this amazing?" with the wide-eyed delight of a child. I was aware of my own cynicism, but I was genuinely surprised that she could find such enchantment in the midst of so much obvious suffering. Didn't she know the history of the place in which she stood? Didn't she know in the square just below, blood ran rivers in the streets in the uprising when the Tibetan people tried to rebel against the Chinese invasion? I mustered some manners and managed an answer to her friendly question. "Yes. It is. I'm also amazed at the change. This was all so different seven years ago."

"Well, change isn't bad, is it?" she said.

I really couldn't answer her. I just shrugged my shoulders and tried to smile. "I guess it depends," I finally said.

I couldn't appreciate it then, but she was right in a sense; enchantment can be found through suffering—it might be the only true way. Sorrow is a sacred blessing, a piercing awl. Depending on one's perspective, through that puncture wound we can choose to see only the loss, what is not there, or look at the opening it has made in us, the spaciousness to be filled up with natural great delight if we are receptive and patient.

YEARS BEFORE, walking the circular road around the Jokang, the shopkeepers were indignant. As I perused the yak-wool sweaters on the tables, they offered me tea and invited me deeper into their shops. They told me stories of the abusive police and government and asked me to tell people at home in the West.

On the terrace of a monastery that I had visited I had seen a monk walking quickly in my direction, his maroon robes snapping in the wind behind him. He had looked straight ahead as he passed me, but he had slipped a note into my hand as he slid by me. The note was printed in English and Tibetan script. It was a paragraph about the human rights abuses going on in the country and a paragraph imploring the reader to report the contents of the note to people in the West.

This time on the streets of Lhasa I saw more Chinese people than Tibetans. The Tibetans I did see were mostly beggars. They didn't pass on notes of resistance and defiance, instead we carried out letters to family for them. They had almost no fight left in them except for the fight to stay alive. They seemed far more subjugated, nearly vanquished. I wondered what that meant for me. Seeing these people so dejected, whom I'd admired because of their tenacity in the face of extreme adversity, I wondered what hope there was for my comparably smaller problem and me. Lhasa, as the Tibetan Shangri-La of centuries ago, is truly gone forever.

Lhasa was the seat of Tibetan Buddhism. Buddhism was the seat of wisdom that had brought me comfort and helped me make sense of everything I experienced. If it could be gone from this place, could it be beaten out of me too by the unrelenting days, lifetimes, crashing in on me? Chris and I finished our tea and talked about the nature of impermanence as the leaves in our pot of tea softened. We talked about Liam and letting go. We talked about email and how no matter where you go these days, you couldn't avoid the cyber-connection to the world. I wondered about a real way to stay connected to the world. Isn't that what we're here for, to make meaningful ties? To come to really know both ourselves and others?

In the street below, a crowd gathered on either side of the main road. We saw a handcuffed monk being walked, with reluctant steps, through the street by the police. I thought it was the same monk we'd seen previously that day running through the Bar-Core trying to evade the police, but maybe it was another one. There was a loudspeaker playing a tape from the police car that followed the monk and his captors. We couldn't understand the Chinese announcement. I asked the waiter who'd come to collect our empty cups what was going on. He told us the announcement said the monk had committed some crime and that he was going to jail. He added that they were going to kill him. I didn't know if he meant to tell me that they were announcing the monk's death too, or if the waiter added his own subtitle to the translation he provided for us.

The politics of the region had not changed that much since 1959, but the attitude of the people had. Existence would not change for me or anyone else; there would always be suffering and attachment. I would always have to strive to find the balance—realize the difference—between tying things together and tying them down.

AFTER A WEEK in Tibet we started to plan our next move. Winter was coming on fast. We knew that we only had a matter of weeks to make the trip overland to Nepal, or we could be snowbound for quite a while since even the flights in and out would slow to a trickle. In all the tourist guest houses there were notes posted from other travelers who were looking to put together a traveling party to keep expenses down. We made the rounds and weighed the options. We decided on a direct route because we found we were too tired for adventure. I really wanted to stop at some sights that were sacred to Tara and the Sakya monastery. Most of our lamas belonged to the Sakya sect of Tibetan Buddhism. Tara was a female deity of compassion. But Chris wanted to move quicker. He wanted to call the Austrian man, Helmut, who posted a sign saying he had rented a car and a driver and was going to drive straight through to Nepal in two days. We met with him and he told us that we would be sharing the car with a Tibetan family as well.

On November 20 we met our group. Helmut introduced us to Lhamo (a Tibetan name meaning "goddess"), her infant son Tenzin ("protector of Dharma"), and her father, whom we all called Pala ("father"). Our driver's name was Tashi ("lucky"). We all squeezed into the Land Rover after our brief introductions and headed out of Lhasa. I was happy to have the company of the Tibetan family. Chris and I tried to practice our Tibetan over the next couple of days. Lhamo seemed pleased to have traveling companions who knew a bit of Tibetan. She smiled when I told her my Tibetan name was Lhamo too. Speaking to her baby, she pointed at me and told him that I was Lhamo and that I was his mother too.

Tenzin was the first baby that I had held since Liam died. Previously, in restaurants, or stores, or on beaches, I would avoid babies. It was too painful to be around them. I was jealous of their mothers and angry that my baby was taken from me. But in this close car, driving through the tall, sheltering Himalayas, I held that small boy—named "the one who protects the teachings"—in my lap and something in me softened because I had no choice, no way to avoid it. His mother-goddess put him on my lap without asking me and before I could refuse him she was nodding and telling him I was a mother-goddess too. I couldn't not close my arms around him, and feel fortunate for the surprising bit of comfort offered to me, and just take in both that and the expansive sky before me as we drove on.

Over the next two days we all took turns holding Tenzin as we bounced over the rocky terrain. I showed Lhamo a picture of my baby that was taped into the journal I kept. She asked me where he was. Was he with my mother, she wanted to know? I tried several times to say the word for dead in Tibetan, but she never understood me. Finally, Chris looked it up in our dictionary and handed it to her, pointing to the word.

"Oh," she said mildly, "I see. He is dead."

"He's dead," Helmut said. "Your baby is dead?" He seemed shocked. "That's awful. What happened to him?"

Chris tried to explain. I hugged Tenzin.

By midday we stopped in a town that was familiar. When I was a student traveling around Tibet, I camped on the roofs of several different monasteries and a nunnery. As my present companions and I untangled our cramped legs from the car, I recognized the monastery on the hill in the distance. At that monastery I had seen a sky-burial. As we headed into a restaurant to order some lunch, I recalled that awe-inspiring event:

THE OTHER STUDENTS and I had arrived in the late afternoon at the monastery. The corpses were already in the middle of the court-yard, and the monks were already gathering for the transfer of consciousness ceremony. As the courtyard began to bustle with activity, I climbed the ladder to the roof where I would be out of the way, but still able to see.

A small fire was lit in front of the corpses. Through the burlap in which they were wrapped, I could make out the form of their bodies. One was large, sitting cross-legged, and doubled over. The second body was smaller and curled in the fetal position. Both bodies were placed with their heads to the fire and *katas*, ceremonial white silk scarves, were tied around their necks. A kata is given to someone as an offering of thanks, a blessing, or for protection on their journey. Katas always bring to my mind scenes of the animated bowing and blessings of tearful departures or long-anticipated arrivals, or the excitement of having received the blessing of a lama. All of these scenes are full of emotion and life.

Seeing katas on corpses made the bodies seem weighted and still heavy with emotion and spirit. The relatives of the dead and the monks were dry-eyed with solemn faces, and their hands were busy with familiar ritual gestures. I couldn't hold back, though. I began to weep for people I'd not known and couldn't even now see except for the outlines of heads, shoulders, and knees bulging from the burlap and tied with rope like packages of meat from a butcher shop.

The monks took their places sitting cross-legged in a semicircle around the bodies. The head lama sat opposite the monks and the corpses on the far side of the fire. The low drone of chanting began and the monks started to slowly rock in meditation to draw out and release the life energy from the bodies. With the repetition of mantras and a certain syllable, *hri*, which emanates special powers, the consciousness of the dead person was transferred to another realm.

The chanting continued until the sun was behind the mountains and the cold night was beginning to settle in. The fire was left to burn out and the bodies were placed in a large wooden crate next to the main entrance to wait for their ultimate disposal and final release.

In the morning I hiked the mile and a half or so to the very top of the mountain to the sky-burial site. By the time I had arrived, the larger of the two bodies had already been destroyed and the relatives were standing or squatting and talking in low murmurs. Some were leaning against the wall of a small stone one-room building. Fifteen to twenty vultures, the smallest of them no less than three feet tall, were already dancing and frenzied as they tried to crowd in near the altar. One man herded them back, waving a large stick, throwing stones, and yelling over the hissing and squawking of the vultures.

The altar was a circle of rocks built up about one foot high and about five feet in diameter. In the field that surrounded the altar there were small stupas draped with red, yellow, blue, green, and white prayer flags. Massive hairy yaks wandered in the distance, inattentive to our gathering.

A monk walked out of the stone building tying on a long white apron stained with spots the color of rotting flesh, rust-red with a tint of green. He took down a large silver hook and a long knife from a hook by the door. He walked to the altar and stood for a minute in silence. Then he began to chant. He walked toward the remaining corpse while the vultures and their guard challenged each other with two steps forward and two steps back.

The wind skimmed over the mountaintop and washed over me. I felt awake. There was no sense of sadness or squeamishness. The knot I thought for sure would be in my throat was not there. I stood quietly, numb, and waited like the relatives, who stood loosely woven together like the knot of interdependence, and silently kicked stones at their feet and shifted their weight back and forth.

The monk raised the hook and brought it down with a sinking *thunk* sound into the back of the corpse and dragged it onto the altar. As he cut away the burlap I could see that the corpse was a woman. She was small, but not frail, with long gray hair and spots of bluish green on her feet where they were beginning to rot. The only cries that could be heard were from the increasingly hungry and aggressive vultures said to be sky *dakinis* who carry the departed up as an offering to the deities. The monk, still chanting, sank the hook into the soles of the corpse's feet, stretched the legs out of the fetal position, and began to cut flesh from bone. My eyes were wide. My heart opened too, sensing the essence of that person had already been carried out the door of this realm the night before on the mantras of the monks and their loved ones.

The bones were nearly scraped clean by the monk's knife when the man with the stick could no longer hold back the vultures. They converged on the altar just as the monk dashed out of the way. They devoured the flesh. Fighting over the larger pieces, they tugged them between their vise-like beaks and picked the bones clean. All the while, their great black wings battered the air with a steady beat like a heart. A small piece of flesh flew up from the carnage and landed on the shoulder of a person who was watching. Another man next to him picked it off nonchalantly and threw it back on the altar, unfazed.

Suddenly, I met the eye of a howling dark dakini/vulture in my own and for a moment I held her gaze unafraid, aware, and amazed. A Tibetan guide warned me to look another way as to not challenge that ferocious and merciful preying creature that sighted me.

The vultures were shooed back from the altar and the monk once again approached. This time he began to crush the bones with a large hammer. When he reached the skull he cut the last patches of hair from it and threw them onto the altar. His chanting grew louder as he set the skull down again. He brought the hammer down with one hard crushing blow then ground the bone and brain into dust. He mixed all the dust with *tsampa*, barley flour. Once again the vultures were allowed to approach.

When the rocks were scavenged bare, they flew away. The people silently dispersed while the monk put away his apron and tools and rewrapped himself in his top robes. I silently walked away, amazed at the sense of calm I felt. Life is not passive and painless, so why should the ritual passage be? Why should it be sanitized and separated from the reality that loss is a crushing blow, a pulverizing agony? Tibetans believe that the body should be returned by means of one of the elements: fire, earth, water, or air. At such high elevations it is hard to find wood enough to consume a body by fire. The ground is so frozen most of the year it is very difficult to dig six feet down. The rivers are few. So there is no choice but to give them back to the sky.

As I walked back to the monastery, past a stupa with flags fluttering and auspicious banners with colorful brocaded lotuses, I looked back. A feeling of peace came over me as I looked out over the Himalayas. That woman was completely free from this world of painful existence. No bone or flesh rotting in the ground to give those left behind a false sense of attachment. No ashes enshrined to weep over. She was well gone anyway before her bones were devoured, so there was no need to be attached to her remains. Material things, flesh and bone included, are an illusion. In the end there is only nothing. One law in all the realms. Impermanance.

A PERSON'S CONSCIOUSNESS is said to remain in an intermediate state called the *bardo* for forty-nine days before the person takes rebirth. On the forty-ninth day after Liam's death, we brought his ashes to Cannon Beach on the Oregon coast. At the Schooner's Cove Inn we set up a shrine next to the sliding glass doors that opened right onto the beach. We made offerings, recited our *sadhanas*, and meditated. According to Jetsun Kusho's instructions we mixed Liam's ashes with fine white porcelain and pressed them into molds called Tsa-tsas, which are little stupas—or canisters that usually hold the relics of lamas and sacred objects.

On the altar I had placed some red roses that I picked from the bushes at home. Liam was born in June and the flower associated with that month is the rose. On the altar I had also lit five candles. They were handmade candles in shades of purples and greens by a brand called Alchemy. Each one was scented and labeled differently; I can recall *amber/cosmic mystery* and *vetiver/tranquility*. I placed our favorite pictures of him there. In three of the seven water-offering bowls I put sand and other simple objects: a Jolly Rancher hard candy and a caramel (one was hard and slippery, the other pliable and sticky, but both were sweet); shells (including one in the shape of a tiny heart I found walking on the beach); and incense, always incense, to carry the prayers to the sky.

And when we were done making the *tsa-tsas* from fine porcelain clay and the ashes of his burned-down bones, I set them on the altar too, like three jewels. I got the blue box in which the funeral home had put Liam's ashes. We lit a small fire on the dusk-robed shore and burned the box.

The next afternoon we took the roses and the *tsa-tsas* out to the beach. We walked a short distance to Haystack Rock, a massive and ancient rock formation just offshore. As the surf rolled in we took turns throwing the *tsa-tsas* as far as we could into the foaming surf. I rolled up the legs of my jeans and let the cold Pacific numb my feet. When the *tsa-tsas* were all gone, I threw in the flowers. I even threw the identification tags from his ashes in the ocean too. On the shore I wrote a note in the sand that read, LIAM, WE LOVE YOU. The tide came in and took back with it the last two words, LOVE YOU; it felt like a response. It left on the shore two words: LIAM and WE. Was it an unfinished sentence or a stating of fact?

"Look what's left," I said to Chris.

As the sun got lower, we walked back toward our motel. We sat on the small patio of our room and opened a bottle of champagne. It was one of two bottles we had saved from our wedding day to drink when our babies were born. In the days just after his birth, so flooded with unexpected trouble, we never drank it. We did toast his one month "birthday" knowing it would be our only one with him. And that night on the coast, as the stars grew brighter over the ocean, on the forty-ninth day after our son's death, we drank a second reverent toast, this time to his fortunate rebirth. We sipped quietly into the night.

...

IN A TOWN near the border of Tibet and Nepal, Chris and I sat in the warm guesthouse below the familiar monastery eating dumplings and tea. When we were all finished we drove the rest of the afternoon until the stars overtook the sky. We slept that night in a guesthouse in Lhatse, Tibet.

Driving the next day, I was struck by how wide and blue the sky was, and endless. When we stopped for lunch, I was approached by a young girl who held her hands out to me. I thought she had a few rocks in her hands, but when I looked closer, I could see that they were nautilus fossils. I asked her in Tibetan as best I could where she had gotten them. Her hand swept over the unending rocky landscape. At one time in geologic history, the top of the world was the bottom of the ocean. We bought two fossils from the girl and I held them in my open hand standing on the open Tibetan plateau. Everything is tied together in some way. I couldn't see the ocean from the Himalayas, but they were still connected. I couldn't hold my son anymore, but he was with me.

We spent our last night in Tibet in the border town of Zhangmu. We had driven as far as we could.

In the morning we walked the last mile or so over the Friendship Bridge into Nepal. We bought a visa from the border guards. We decide to forgo the bus to Kathmandu and splurge on a taxi instead. We bargained the driver down to two thousand rupees, which was the exact amount of rupees I had left over from my previous trip.

As we descended in altitude, we shed layers of clothing. It seemed my sullen attitude was melting away too. The mountains dwindled to a fraction of their size. The snow receded to reveal green leaves. Winter melted away before my eyes. I felt better than I had in days. Our driver, Krishna, had a broad, white smile that reminded me of the glaciers we had just come over. He was very friendly. We communicated not with words, because we didn't share a language, but with gestures. We stopped a few times throughout the daylong drive. Krishna's brother, who was along for the ride, bought some small, sweet oranges from a roadside vendor and shared them with us. We stopped for tea and all drank a cup. As the men smoked bidi cigarettes, I squatted and helped a Nepalese woman with lovely bright eyes sort stones from a wide bowl of rice. In the car, when we continued driving, Chris conveyed to Krishna that he liked the music he was playing, and Krishna turned it louder. We were a brought-together-by-chance parade in one vehicle, and the sound of tablas and sitars swelled around us as dusk came on.

As we approached Outer Ring Road and Kathmandu, I saw a circus in a distant field. The houses and the people swelled up like waves on the shore as we approached the sea of humanity that has been pooling at the base of the great Tibetan plateau for millennia.

Small Votives and Veils of Smoke

In the middle of the journey of our life I came to myself
within a dark wood where the straight way was lost.
—*Dante Alighieri*

W E HADN'T YET MADE ARRANGEMENTS for a hotel in
Kathmandu. Krishna said he'd take us to his friend's
hotel. We wound our way through the narrow streets of
Kathmandu's old city, Chhetrapati. Everywhere I looked the shops
and homes were lit by candles. Warm yellow light filtered out
through the intricately carved wooden shutters. Pathways were lit by
twinkling votives. The glow gave a gentle feeling to a city with rough
and ancient edges. I knew from experience that this was yet another
power outage and there was no way to know when the light would
return. "*Kay garney*" is a phrase that the Nepalese use often. It literally translates to "What can you do?" It seems often to mean something more like "There is nothing to be done, so don't worry so
much; just let it be."

People passed close to the cab's windows carrying lanterns that
lit only portions of their faces; in the shadowy glow they appeared

skeletal. It felt as if we had driven not only from Tibet to Kathmandu but back to an ancient time. I realized that many people had passed through these streets over many lifetimes. There was not one of them who could give me a mustard seed like the one that the devastated mother who went to the Buddha searched for. In each of those homes and shops that had stood for thousands of years, a light had gone out. For generations in those homes, people lit candles on their altars for the brothers, and mothers, and daughters, and sons who had passed.

We had no services when Liam passed. We waked him the only way we could at the time, instinctively, setting an altar in our front room where anyone would see it upon entering our home, keeping his presence with us the only way possible—symbolically, elliptically—and then, to go on living anyway.

When we arrived at the Hotel Harati, which was very nice with a driveway and marble lobby, we knew right away that it would be more expensive than we had intended to pay. But we decided to at least go in and check the price. Luckily bargaining is a way of life in Asia. The pleasant front counter man told us the price per night was sixty U.S. dollars. I explained to him that we were sorry, but we'd have to go somewhere else because it was more than we could afford. He said, with a smile, "How much do you want to pay, madam?" He agreed to thirty a night without dickering on price. We checked in.

I was happy to be staying in such a luxurious hotel. The room was clean with a toilet rather than two porcelain footprints on either side of a hole over a pipe for a toilet, and it had a Western shower instead of a showerhead attached to the middle of the wall without any basin or curtain to contain the water. Even though Chris thought thirty dollars was too expensive for our budget, we decided we'd stay at least a night or two to refresh ourselves. I had a shower and soaked in the hot water and candle-glow that lit the white-tiled room. We went to the restaurant on the main floor that overlooked a wide green lawn surrounded by a tropical garden. It felt like an oasis. We ordered dinner. I even had a whiskey sour, which seemed very posh for Kathmandu and the kind of travel to which we were accustomed.

Walking through the candle-lit lobby to the restaurant, I had picked up a brochure for the hotel, which I was in the habit of doing because I pasted bits and pieces—business cards, sugar packets, postcards, and used train tickets—into my journal. The brochure told the legend of the deity Harati. I felt like we had come to the right place, and that we were on the right path.

According to the brochure, Harati is a benevolent spirit connected to earthly fertility. She lived in the time of Shakyamuni Buddha. Her love for children overflowed the bounds of her own family and drove her to kidnap children and take them away to an enchanted garden where she told them amazing stories. The distraught parents of the missing children appealed to the Buddha. To make Harati realize the pain she had been causing, he arranged for her favorite child to be taken away, making sure that Harati knew that it was the Buddha who had taken her child. Very quickly Harati realized what the Buddha was trying to teach her, and she went to him and begged him to give her child back. He did, of course, but he also reprimanded her for taking the other children. She realized her mistake and returned the children, but she asked the Buddha to make her a special protector of all children. Buddha granted her request and made her the patroness of children and protectress of his holy places. Her shrines stand next to the great Buddhist monuments of the Kathmandu Valley. Parents still invoke her patronage and protection for their children.

The brochure said that Harati's most sacred shrine was on Swayambhu's Hill, not too far from the hotel. When we got to our room after dinner I remembered to look out the window and check the view. There was an obscured view of Swayambhu's Hill. Like that view, the correct worldview is sometimes obscured. I was trying hard to see past my own pain, but everywhere I looked I saw the pain of others, and it wasn't any easier to take. In fact, it was beginning to overwhelm me even in such a lovely place. I thought I should become like Harati, find a way to help children and other parents who had lost children.

I loved that she was a storyteller too.

But I had no idea how to help myself or anyone else.

CHRIS AND I had been in Kathmandu together before. Several years earlier, after my Tibetan studies program ended, Chris came over to meet me. We barely knew each other and had no idea that we'd get married and have a son. We never would've imagined that we'd be back in Kathmandu again after his death. In our travels so far, this was the first country that we had been to in which we shared a history: being young and in love and childless. Seven years later we'd had a child, but we were childless. We were still young and still in love, but we were struggling to make love be enough to keep us together when the sadness we both felt was pushing us apart.

I was reminded of being with Chris at a time when every hair on his head was not familiar to me as it was now. I remembered looking at him and just seeing his face. Now when I looked at him I could hardly see him at all. I saw Liam. Some days I couldn't take my eyes off of him because it was a comfort. Other days I could barely look at him because it was such a painful reminder. Some days, longing and grief turned into anger that I turned on Chris. We fought a lot, not about anything real but about things like money or where to have lunch. He was so afraid to run out of money, to be left with nothing, to be stuck in the middle of nowhere. What I now realized was that maybe the money was just a substitute for him to hold on to; one thing, at least, which he could control.

He wasn't really afraid to run out of money. I think he was afraid to feel what was already true. If he could keep us from running out of money then maybe he could emotionally reverse the reality that we had already lost everything, that we were emotionally, and almost spiritually, bankrupt.

In Kathmandu we wandered the streets trying to find our way to houses and teashops we lived in and remembered. I recalled the feelings I had there before our present trip: feeling hopeful, and energized, and alive. We met with old home-stay families and friends who had stayed behind to live in Nepal after we returned to college. I was reminded of who we used to be.

I just wanted comfort, and I didn't care what it cost. Running out of money and having to go home early seemed a small price to pay if I could be happy again, even if the happiness lasted only as long as a hot bath. But I knew it was important to Chris, so I agreed to change hotels, to exchange the luxury of a carpeted room with a proper bed, drapes, and toilet for the friendly but exceptionally no-frills room at Mom's House Lodge.

It was an unheated cinderblock room. There were two beds with straw mattresses covered by wool blankets, and no sheets. We would use our sleeping bags to stay warm. We did splurge and get a room with an attached bathroom of the standard Nepalese variety that included a squat-a-potty and an open shower. And it was fine. I liked that it made Chris happy to be saving money. I liked the simplicity of the room. It felt minimalist. We could get by, make do, not be so attached. I loved that at the bottom of the entrance steps a man sat every day selling incense. As I came and went, I had to walk through a cloud of billowing, perfumed smoke. The fragrant white curtain reminded me of the veil between this life and the next. It reminded me that life can be smoke—fragrant incense rising, an offering.

The day before Thanksgiving, as we were leaving Mom's Lodge, a familiar man was walking toward me. I recognized him before he recognized me, so he was more startled than I was when we came together in the street and I called his name. He was a colleague from the bookstore I had quit. It was strange that again we were running into people from our lives in Oregon no matter how far away we went.

When I was pregnant with Liam and still at the largest independent bookstore in Portland, I had worked hard to be eligible for a promotion. I interviewed for a position in the public relations department of which this colleague who was now strolling Kathmandu's streets was the head. He called to offer me the position I desperately wanted a few days after Liam passed away. I went to his office and said that I really wanted the job but I couldn't start right away because I needed some time. I asked if I could start in a couple of months. He said he couldn't wait because the holidays were coming up and he needed everyone there in the store. I decided not to take the promotion.

Seeing him standing right smack in front of me as I left the guest lodge the day before Thanksgiving was a shocking reminder of what I'd given up as well as lost. I tried to trust that I made the right choice to quit my job and travel around the world. I tried to trust that there was a reason I was on that path at that time. I tried to be thankful for what I did have. I had amazing experiences and good teachers; I had the path ahead and company on it. And I had choices to make. In the darkness I had stars to look up to.

In Mom's House one night I had a dream of Sogyal Rinpoche. The details are smoke-like now except for the strong feeling I can still recall of waking to his dream-presence as if I were receiving a direct transmission. He told me the greatest quality a person could cultivate wasn't wisdom or compassion, but courage.

Eventually I understood the dream better. Everyone has wisdom and compassion, but whether it is smoldering in the dark or bright like star-fire depends on courage. Do I have the courage to seek wisdom and compassion in others and myself? Do I have the courage to dwell in the wisdom mind if I can cultivate it? Am I courageous enough when the path seems very dark to stay on it and discover what startling truth lies ahead?

The Charnel Ground

> Chaos is part of our home ground. Instead of looking for
> something higher or purer, work with it just as it is . . . the
> chaos in here and the chaos out there is basic energy, the
> play of wisdom . . . the basis of freedom and the basis of
> confusion . . . This charnel ground called life is the
> manifestation of wisdom.
> —*Pema Chödrön*

WE PLANNED TO GO TO INDIA TO SEE some of the
Buddha's holy places like Lumbini, where he was born;
and Bodhgaya, where he found enlightenment under an
acacia tree; and Sarnath, where he gave his first teaching, and turned
the Wheel of Dharma for the first time.

We didn't plan to stay in Varanasi, but it was a good place to start
since it was central to the places we wanted to visit and the air ticket
there was cheap. We managed to find our way by bus and taxi to the
Dashashwameda Ghat in the old city near the burning *ghats*, concrete platforms with steps leading down into the Ganges River on
which funeral pyres are built. During a funeral the steps are painted

brightly and lit with thousands of candles. Dashashwameda is one of the oldest funeral *ghats* in one of the oldest cities on earth. The Ganges, and the burning *ghats* on it, is one of the most sacred places on earth for Hindus. Many old people give up all their possessions and go to live the last days of their lives on the banks of the Ganges bathing in her waters and praying. Corpses bound in cloth and draped in marigolds and carnations are carried daily on the shoulders of their families to the burning pyres on the *ghats*. Their bodies are consumed in the flames stoked with incense and prayer. The ashes are gathered and then scattered in the flowing waters where they mingle with the ashes of millions. We had no ashes to add to the river, only tears and wishes.

I was a pyre—a combustible heap, consumed by chaos, and confused.

WHEN WE GOT OUT OF THE TAXI, young men wanting to carry our bags for a fee swarmed us. We felt we could manage, but we accepted the offer of one of the boys in the crowd to lead us to a guesthouse so he could collect a fee from the owner.

"Right this way. Just ahead. Very good place," were the things he said over his shoulder as he turned every so often, enticing us not to give up as we wound through the narrow streets that felt like gangways between the brick buildings. Arriving at the Yogini Guest House, we settled into our budget-minded room, about a dollar a night. There were two rope cots with straw mattresses and no sheets. To make it feel more homey and to freshen the air of the dank, closed room I lit some incense that I had bought from the man at the bottom of the stairs in Kathmandu. I laid out my sleeping bag and set my pack on the bed for a pillow.

I was starting to feel as old as what Mark Twain had written about Varanasi: "It is older than history, older than tradition, even older than legend, and it looks twice as old as all of them put together."

Not far from the Yogini was another guesthouse called the Vishnu that had a veranda that overlooked the Ganges. I spent a good part of the first couple of days sitting there drinking tea, reading, and pasting together a patchwork of memories from torn bits of fliers, maps, postcards, and notes in my journal. The tearing, and pasting, and piecing together occupied my mind. The scraps were shattered bits of my days, and I was trying to put them together to make sense, to glue down the memories before they faded, to make some kind of mosaic beauty of the chaos. The whole trip, I was obsessed with collecting, and pasting, and preserving.

I guess this book—the one you are holding now, the one that grew from my journal which reflected my mosaic, mending mind— is Liam's baby-book, a scraped-together keepsake of him, and a testimony of my ever-present obsession of sensing his spirit, even though I feel his absence. It's a documentary of incidents that made an impression on me, valuable moments that informed my journey, flashes of lightning, dark clouds, glints of sun on water, crashing waves, and realizing—at the exact moment needed—how beautiful it is that rare Tibetan blue poppies exist at all.

WHILE SIPPING HOT SWEET TEA at the Vishnu just after sunset one faded day, off in the distance on the Ganges, I saw the silhouette of several people, illuminated by lantern light, in a small boat. They lit small candles and set them adrift on the Ganges. The shore was teeming with worshipers as well. I watched as the boat drifted past me in the distance with the quick current, leaving a trail of fire in the water behind it. Liam was perfect and severely damaged all at the same time.

I could love him, and I could let him go too.

Fire could float on water.

...

SARNATH was a relatively short distance from Varanasi so we were able to make a day trip to visit the place where Buddha gave his first teaching. The small community was quiet and clean compared to the gangways of Varanasi that were bursting with people, and dirt, and dogs, and noise. We spent a relaxing day walking around. Years ago, on the same trip when Chris and I were in Nepal together, we had attended a Kalachakra teaching in Varanasi given by His Holiness the Dalai Lama. At that time the small holy city was teeming with people young and old, foreign trekkers and indigenous dwellers mingled in with the sea of monks and nuns attired in maroon and saffron robes, some of whom carried parasols of the same colors to protect them from the relentless sun. We were all there for the same thing, to receive the teaching and view the sacred Kalachakra sand mandala of peace.

The Kalachakra mandala, which is a symbolic representation of the sacred mansion of a deity, has several circular borders with a series of boxes layered and nesting one in another like a child's stacking blocks. The boxes represent the realms of existence and realms of body, and speech, and mind, and wisdom with great bliss.

Throughout my journey I kept noticing boxes: small wooden boxes with all that I had left, box hedges beyond a boxy desk, a box of bones, boxes transformed into altars, boxes people carried, and boxes that contained me, white boxy restaurants where I drank Tibetan tea as tantalizing as sacred dreams. It's only now, looking back, I begin to see the possibility that I was walking, as I made my way around the world and as I continue to walk everyday, through a mandala, which is a house with sacred rooms: the room of wisdom and bliss housed within the room of the mind, within the room of the speech, within the room of the body. The universe is the house—a spirit motel—and within these ordinary and universal rooms and days there lives a deity of wisdom and bliss. Maybe there's a universe in me.

Just seeing the Kalachakra mandala can bring a person peace and plant a seed that will have a karmic effect. Recalling that initiation and being in Sarnath again, an oasis of calm in a crowded and chaotic country, was soothing. But, just like it's so hard to truly enter and stay in the mansion of the aware and meditative mind, we found we were soon on the outside again.

IN THE RICKSHAW that we had hired to drive us home that evening, I went to pieces again. Our driver had stopped for the third time to make repairs to his bike for which he insisted we pay. Night was coming on. Being in a dark and unfamiliar place terrified me. I had no idea how far we were from the guesthouse. I felt like we were at the driver's mercy.

"At this rate the driver will construct a whole new bike, part by part, before we get back," I sarcastically joked with Chris.

I tried to control my growing panic, but my skin began to tingle as if I were going numb except for the tightness in my chest. A man approached our rickshaw and leaned on the driver's bike seat staring at me unabashed. I couldn't breathe. Chris leaned back to avoid him, leaving me fully exposed.

"What are you doing, Chris?" I yelled.

"What do you mean?" Chris shot back.

"Do something."

"What?"

"Anything. Something. Make him go away," I said. "You could at least lean forward to block his view."

Sighing, Chris tried to put himself between the man and me. The man just craned his neck around Chris.

"Leave me alone." I yelled at the man. I motioned with my hand for him to leave, but he just smiled and chortled as if I were some amusing caged animal.

"What do you want me to do," Chris said. "I don't want to fight with him." Finally the driver was ready to go. We left the man by the side of the road. The terror stayed with me.

"I don't want to go to Bodhgaya or anyplace else in India with you," I told Chris.

The men in India could be invasive and rude. It felt like a lot of them had no respect for women at all. Traveling there before, and now, I'd been grabbed and groped by their prodding eyes and their rough hands. I felt like I had no strength to fend them off myself this time. I felt like Chris would not protect me either. He thought I was being unreasonable, and maybe I was. Maybe that's not what I was mad about. Maybe the leering man was an incarnation of death that had stood by my side from the moment that Liam was born. It wasn't logical that Chris could divert the staring eyes of a whole country any more than he could protect us, or Liam, from death. These thoughts didn't occur to me sitting in the rickshaw as my skin crawled and the leering emanation of death, disguised as an indifferent man with penetrating eyes, stared at me, looking in, I imagined, to my pounding heart, ready to rip it out just as death had stood by for a little over a month that my son lived.

We rode in silence the rest of the way back to the guesthouse. The darkness closed around us. Yellow light from the kerosene lanterns spilled out of the many stalls along the roads where shop-keepers sat cross-legged on wooden platforms staring out and wait-ing to measure off portions of *garam masala*, saffron, or silk.

TAKING A WALK, on a later day, I was alarmed as I passed through the jammed corridors heading back to the guesthouse from a ven-ture I tried to take alone on the Ganges that was thwarted by a foul-mouthed teenager; I couldn't help but think on my brooding walk back what a waste it was that he had the ability to think and articu-late and he betrayed that gift by taunting people with lascivious and disrespectful comments and questions.

In the distance I could see that the people were clearing a path for something to pass. Everyone fell silent as they moved to one side or the other, clinging to the rough stone buildings as if they couldn't get clear enough from what was moving by them. The crowd split in front of me. A man swaddled in a white shawl and Punjabi (a tunic and baggy pants) led a muzzled creature that I'd never seen before by a rope leash toward me in the wake of the crowd. I couldn't identify the animal I saw coming toward me. It was not taller than a full-grown hog, but was as burly and hairy as a brown bear. I jumped into a doorway as it approached. Because I couldn't take my eyes off the animal, I knocked down an old woman who was in front of me. I stooped to help her up as the creature passed. Everyone on the street was silent and staring. It seemed that if the animal wanted to break free there would be little chance that the man and his short rope could hold it back. Its size, about half as tall as the man, its dark eyes, the way it slightly bucked at the muzzle, suggested it was capable of great harm. Later I learned that the animal I saw was a wolverine, which is said to be the fiercest animal on earth.

After the people in the narrow street began to move again, I continued on to the guesthouse. I turned a corner into a darker alleyway that led away from the crowd. I watched my swollen feet, stepping over litter and piles of shit and a stagnant puddle with a dead rat. I realized, looking at the filth at my feet, that that was all I'd been looking at for days. I was unable to look up for very long at the path in front of me. When I did force myself to look up, imbedded in the vendor's colorful displays of fruit, and silk, and incense, and tea, and glass bangles, and fresh vegetables, I saw old people who were dying, beggars with weeping sores, children who were stunted and shrunken by hunger. The ancient city, the sacred place where people came to leave their dead, was pressing in on me. Inside I felt like my mind was becoming a dark creature unknown to me.

I was tethered and in control, but only by a short rope of willpower that might not be enough.

FOR THE NEXT THREE DAYS I couldn't leave my bed. I was delirious with fever. I only got up to squat or retch in the bathroom a few feet from my bed. When I was awake I watched a little mouse that scurried around the room, or the moon that would pass slowly over the carved wooden shutter. Chris came back to the room several times to check on me. Once he brought me some chicken and *naan*, round flat bread cooked in a tandoor oven, but I wasn't able to eat. I lived on Cipro, an anti-diuretic, and water.

On the third day of my incapacitating bout with what was probably amoebic dysentery, the toilet pipe backed up, filling the bathroom an inch deep. We called the manager to come to the room to fix it. He said he would go get someone from the lower caste to clean it. He made a joke that they would touch anything. The lowest caste in India is said to be "untouchable." Orphans too are said to be untouchable, because of their great misfortune that caused them to lose their parents. I felt untouchable too.

Kids who lose parents have a name. Husbands and wives who lose their spouses have a name. What do you call parents who lose their babies? It's an unnamed, and mostly unvoiced, situation of despair. We might call ourselves the Blue Poppy parents, the ones who have seen our children flower, for no matter how small an amount of time, and die. We are in a despair that often feels ineffable, which closes us into an unseen, unaddressed, sometimes uncomforted, community. The name widow or orphan at least recognizes the beloved person who lived.

I felt an unspeakable conflict when someone asked me after Liam died if I had children. I had to choose between saying no, which seemed to betray Liam's life, or saying yes, but he died—

leaving me stuck in an awkward situation because most people don't know what to say or how to respond to an answer like that. Sometimes people say, "what a horrible experience that must have been," with, of course, every intention of trying to sympathize. And again, if I say yes, I betray the great love and beauty and delight of him that came hand-in-hand with the horror of his diagnosis and passing. If I said no, not horrible, I was afraid I'd seem indifferent, or crazy, or cold-hearted.

Wouldn't it be nice if the morticians gave out blue poppy pins for us to wear instead of empty, ceramic hearts—a small symbol that says what needs to be said in a way that lets us all be at ease, just like the words orphan or widow do? And better, if we knew to say something like, "That must have been a powerful/moving/intense experience for you." All of those descriptions would be more true than horrible. All people, no matter how small, all lives, no matter for how short or long they bloom, are full of power. Blue poppies take root in mountainous scree; there is a place for happiness in the hard conversations of loss.

Now that the rooftop of the world has been explored and exported, some initiates inclined to cultivate rare plants have made blue poppies more prevalent. It's been rare for us parents to speak of our loss, which was thought also to be rare. Now, with care, the memory of these delicate and powerful lives, our Blue Poppy Babies, can be brought into the light, and we can see we're not alone. We can talk about them, openly, who they were and what they meant to us. To be able, to feel allowed, to talk about our Blue Poppy children *joyfully* is even more rare then talking about losing them. Our kind of loss is more common than most people know. And more complex.

There is a bright center in all that darkness of my loss that speaks to me still. Liam's existence makes me consider this moment now, consider the blessing of time, and consider the power of wisdom and skillful means.

Liam taught me just by being there. By existing. And despite his limitations and everything against him. On the phone one day my grandma told me she was praying for a miracle. "He already is a miracle," I told her quietly, not knowing how to explain what I meant any more than that. We are all miracles, aren't we? That we are here at all, maybe that should tell us something. Maybe we are all small miracles, chaos of matter, capable of birthing light even with our limitations. My heart broke because of that powerful experience of Liam's short life, but it broke it open too.

It's not just that I loved my son; when Liam was here, in concert with the crushing dread, I simply loved, unstrained and easily, without reservation, without discernment, without judgment, I was open to almost everyone that I encountered. To live in love and to gratefully accept the world with all its awful, unspeakable blessings was a sacred experience. What was solely horrifying was what came after the time with Liam when he revealed to me how to live within a spacious mind. Having to go on living, which is no small matter, and move on, through the chaos in here and out there. And knowing what a struggle it will be since I'm intensely aware that I'm not able every day to evoke this understanding he drew out of me and not give in to my horrible nature that comes hand in hand with my loving one.

THERE WAS NO OTHER SUITABLE ROOM in the Yogini for us to move to. It was clear that the filth that had backed up into our room wouldn't be cleaned and fixed for some unknowable amount of time. What did that signify? Move on or be flooded with thoughts, feelings, emotions that I'd painfully been trying to purge? Maybe I couldn't bear the emotional toll any more of my grief. I literally couldn't keep anything down. Every chaotically painful emotion was coming up. I had no bones or ashes to deliver to that charnel ground, but maybe I did indeed have something to leave there. I was falling to pieces like the chopped-up corpses that the ancient yogis sought out to help them turn their understanding inside-out, allowing them to accept death and decay as a manifestation of wisdom just as much as all the nourishing and delightful things in life are.

We moved to the Ajay guesthouse, a short walk away that was situated right on the Ganges and had a nice rooftop view of the city and the river.

The next morning I felt well enough to join Chris on the rooftop café and try to eat some tea and toast. It was nice, but there was a group of monkeys that had staked their claim. They would swing down from the nearby trees, scamper over the rooftop and snatch food from the tables and jump on people. More than losing food or a pen from the table, I was afraid of being bitten.

Their screeching pinched my nerves. It was impossible to sit still and relax because I was constantly looking over my shoulder, afraid for a wild animal to attack. Another traveler who must have been staying there for some time, at least long enough to devise a plan to deal with the monkeys, had a cap gun. Every so often when the monkeys got too close to his breakfast, he picked it up and fired it into the air. The Monkey-Gun Man helped a young boy from the guesthouse fly a kite in between bites and shots. Chris and I passed some time chatting with the other guests, but I felt unsettled.

Chris and I talked about a plan for the next few days; where we would go next and how we would get there. I'm not sure what it was that broke the short tether reining in my mind like a wild elephant. The boy let out the slack on the kite; it sailed up into the blue sky.

The man fired another shot, and, though I can't remember what it was, made a comment so horrifying, I remember it made me gasp, and I bolted out of my chair and ran down the steps. I couldn't stop myself from running. I had to get out of Varanasi.

Chris ran behind me. "What's wrong? Wait! Stop!"

"I can't take this. I'm leaving. I have to leave." I repeated the phrase like a counterproductive mantra and kept running. I started to pack my bag immediately and frantically once I reached the room.

"Just calm down. We'll go, just calm down so we can make a plan." Chris agreed to leave, though I'd still not given him a sane reason. I paced the room like a wolverine, trying to restrain with my pacing a wild-animal of anger. I tried to steady my hyperventilation, pushing my palms into the sockets of my eyes, and moaning, "I can't do this, I can't do this." I was saying I couldn't let go, couldn't go on.

"Do what?" Chris was exasperated and impatient.

"I don't know." I yelled. "I don't know how to live without Liam."

I didn't think I could break open any further and so I ran, instinctively. I wasn't brave enough to abide and come totally undone and be consumed by a wretchedness that was completely mine, and ancient too.

IT WAS 8 AM. We went to the travel agency we saw near the Yogini guesthouse. The agent told us that there was only one train a week to Lumbini, but luckily it was the right day; it would be leaving late that afternoon. He told us we needed to go to the train station to buy the ticket. When we got there the man at the ticket window said that the train had no first-class accommodations. I didn't think I could take an eleven-hour train ride in a crowded third-class car, so we didn't buy tickets.

By the time we got back to the agency to see what other plans we could make, it was 3 PM. The agent told us the options we had for flying further south in India. We also asked about going north to Delhi where we could pick up the next leg of our round-the-world tickets and continue on to Germany. We weighed our options. The next flight to Delhi, connecting to Frankfurt, would be leaving at 4:20 PM.

We decided to try, even though it seemed impossible that we'd be able to make it given the pace of life in India, which requires, sometimes, a half hour to get a cup of tea. We paid for the tickets anyway and ran back to the hotel to get our packs while the agent called to get us a taxi. When we got back to the agent, we groaned when he told us that the airport was about an hour away and we'd have to stop on the way to pick up the nonrefundable tickets. Our plan seemed doomed, but we hopped in the cab and hoped for the best.

The streets were clogged. We were at a standstill not five minutes into the ride. I reminded the driver that we had less than an hour to catch a plane. He somehow made his way through the intersection clogged with people, rickshaws, cows, and vendors with their carts. He picked up speed and started driving fast.

"We'll either be dead in a car accident or on the plane, but either way we'll be leaving India today," I joked to Chris. And either way would be fine with me, I thought. When the driver stopped to pick up the ticket, he told us that the flight had been delayed until 4:50 PM, which gave us some hope. We got to the airport just in time to walk onto the plane as they shut the door behind us. My seat was on the aisle. I didn't mind not having a window; I'd seen enough. I shut my eyes as the plane took off and climbed.

When we got to Delhi we had some time before our connection. I was feeling less panicked and started to feel bad that Chris had to give up his plans for continued travel in India. Part of me also wanted to stay and go south. I wanted to see the Buddha's holy shrines. I also really wanted to go to the Maldive Islands and explore the Kerala region of India, which is supposed to be so beautiful.

"I don't know, Chris," I said. "Maybe we should fly to Kerala."

"You need to decide, Katie," he sighed. "I don't want you to get mad at me if we go south and you're miserable."

We asked at the ticket counter about the price and available flights. Before I could make up my mind, my gut made the decision for me. It was wrenching again and I needed to vomit. I didn't feel in any condition to take on India and its mixed bag of agony and delights any longer.

What I Practiced For

This existence of ours is as transient as autumn clouds.
To watch the birth and death of beings is like looking at
the movements of a dance. A lifetime is like a flash of
lightning in the sky. Rushing by, like a torrent down
a steep mountain.
—*The Buddha,* Lalitavistara Sutra,
translated by Gwendolyn Bays

BEING PREGNANT WITH LIAM had been like desperately
wanting something and having it all at the same time. When I
looked in the mirror, for a change, I liked what I saw. My perception of self changed as I changed from the inside out. There were
no complications, yet, and I felt strong once the constant vomiting
and exhaustion of the first trimester subsided.

Work had become extremely busy with an impending special
event and author appearances of which I was in charge. The stress
of the long hours spent on my feet began to take its toll. At six
months the exhaustion and vomiting of the early months of pregnancy returned. My nurse/midwife suggested I reduce my hours at

work, and I did, despite pangs of guilt for not being stronger. Fewer hours allowed me to get in some extra swimming. I craved floating weightless in the water.

I read every book I could find on pregnancy and natural childbirth; that's what I was planning on. I skipped all the small sections in every book about complications. I wasn't planning on having any of those. Chris and I took birthing classes, practiced birthing positions, and learned all the techniques for handling a totally natural childbirth. We learned all the right questions to ask to avoid any unnecessary interventions. Is mom okay? Is baby okay?

We had been totally unprepared. The classes and the readings had not prepared us for what would happen if the answer to those questions was no.

I HAD ALWAYS DREAMED of being a mom. As I grew out and the due date grew nearer I struggled with the dream and the reality of being "just a mom." I daydreamed about staying home even as I worked toward a promotion at the bookstore. Mid-term, I wasn't yet ready to decide.

I had other dreams too. Not dreams of ambition about work and self-definition, but real in-the-dark-night-dowsing-the-future dreams. These are the ones I remember: I was in labor. I was calling for help but no one came in time. I delivered the baby myself, but the baby is only "half-done," I thought; it had a tail like a mermaid.

I dreamed of labor often. I was usually calling for help. I dreamed of the Dalai Lama and other high lamas often. They offered me food and invited me to be near them. I didn't place too much import on the dreams at the time. I had been attending many teachings, and I chalked the dreams up to residue of the teachings at play in my midnight mind.

I had other fears too. Instead of attributing them to nightmares I assigned them a hormonal origin. Once I was hysterical because I knew that one day my baby would want to go to the park alone, and I wouldn't be able to protect him. I cried fearing my breasts weren't shaped right, which might make nursing difficult. I was sure that my baby wouldn't be able to eat because of me. "I won't be able to feed him," I told Chris one night when I was crying in bed and he asked what I was afraid of. I also told him I was afraid of the pain and how much it was going to hurt. "It won't be that bad," he said, but we both laughed, knowing there was no way a pregnant woman can avoid pain.

On June 10 Chris and I went to see our midwife for my thirty-ninth-week check-up. For the second week in a row my blood pressure was slightly elevated, but she wasn't alarmed because the week before my blood and urine had already been tested to rule out any complications. The tests all came back perfect. At the end of the visit she tested my blood pressure again to see if it had come down like it did the week before. She also had another listen with the Doppler.

We heard the baby's heartbeat decelerate at the exact moment we happened to listen. Our midwife was cautious. She wanted a reading from a monitor before I left the office to check for fetal heart-rate and movement. The technician adjusted the monitor a couple of times; with her hands she shook my belly vigorously. The baby's heart was beating. But the baby was too still. Unresponsive.

Our midwife wanted to admit me to the hospital across the street to be monitored. She reassured us and we tried not to be alarmed. At the entrance to the hospital I pulled on Chris's arm.

"I just want to stop here." I wanted to take a quiet second or two to acknowledge, "When we go through those doors everything will be different. When we come out we will have our baby. I know she isn't going to let us leave until our baby is born one way or another."

"I know," Chris agreed.

Holding hands as the automatic glass doors opened before us, we went in together.

Early the next morning we agreed to the labor induction advised by our midwife, who since yesterday's events was consulting on our care with an OB/GYN partner in her practice. As my contractions came on stronger over the next few hours, our baby's heartbeat got weaker. After every contraction his heart was decelerating more. While the midwife and the OB/GYN stood by my bedside the baby's heart took a turn for the worse, which the doctor could see reflected on the monitoring strip. "We have to deliver him now," she said. In less than a half hour I was prepped to go under the knife, and four minutes after that on June 11, 1998, Liam Christopher Morton was born at 6:09 PM.

When they took him out of me on the operating table, he needed to be resuscitated. The pediatrician, and nurses, and attendants worked methodically on him. Chris hovered over the warming bed that Liam was lying on. I was still being sewn back together, vomiting and shivering on the table under the bright surgical lights. They were so busy I had to ask if it was a boy or a girl. They held him up to my lips so that I could give him a kiss. I'd never felt any happiness to compare to the saturating bliss when my lips first touched his forehead, so warm and soft it felt like kissing a rose petal in the sun. Then they handed him to his father who carried him directly to the intensive care unit. Liam didn't cry; he never moved. The doctors didn't know what was wrong with him so they waited, and we waited.

It was hours before I could see him again. I couldn't move my legs due to the spinal block they had given me before the C-section.

I kept trying to wiggle my toes, desperate to make them move. I was still in a morphine-induced state of mind that kept me from comprehending Liam's dire condition. I was aware of only my euphoria because my wished-for baby was finally in the world. Finally, around 11:00 PM, my legs had enough feeling that I could move them. I had to get up; I couldn't go to sleep without seeing him. I could feel the blood drain from my face. I heard the nurse say to someone, "Get the smelling salts." I made it to the wheelchair beside my bed without blacking out, but I had to sit very still and let the wave of nausea and dizziness wash over me. Chris wheeled me very slowly into the intensive care nursery.

I knew instantly when I saw Liam that he was in trouble. I put my hand on his head and exhaled. I heard very clearly a voice in my head say, He is going to die, and we are going to have to start over. I was afraid. The thought was so loud I thought I actually said it. I was ashamed by the morbid thought that shot through me. I took his hand, unfurling his long slender fingers, and wrapped them around mine.

On Saturday somewhere in the dawn hours the nurse and doctor came to my room and asked me to come to the nursery right away. Despite the sleeping pill I took because I hadn't slept in three days, I was alarmed and awake right away. Liam had begun to have seizures and they needed to transfer him to the NICU at Emmanuel Hospital across town. Chris went with Liam in the ambulance. My mother, who had arrived from Chicago a couple of hours before Liam was born, helped me pack my things and drove me over there too.

We stayed on the unit with Liam for a week. Three meetings punctuated the whole experience in the NICU:

LATE IN THE AFTERNOON on the day Liam was transferred, we were called to a meeting with the neonatologist, the cardiologist, the cardiac surgeon, and the neurologist who were all assessing Liam's conditions and ready to give us the diagnosis. The prognosis was not good; it was the unthinkable worst. Liam had a fatal heart condition. They could operate, but he might die, and they couldn't repair the severe brain damage that was already done. They doubted he would be able to think. Later when I read the doctors' reports they put it even more clinically, "Liam's condition is not conducive with life."

Our lama, whom we called Geshe-la, came to the hospital to give Liam a blessing. He held my hands as I cried and he reminded me to have courage. I asked him what mantras I should recite, and he said I could say some Tara mantras if it made me feel better, but that didn't matter so much. "This is the Dharma," he said. "This is what you practice for."

While I was pregnant with Liam we had been attending teachings with Geshe-la. At the last teaching we attended, before Liam's birth, Geshe-la spoke about a chapter that described what happens when we lose control of ourselves. Our minds become like a herd of wild elephants stampeding madly, causing great harm and danger. Geshe-la told me to have control, and to have courage. Those words were the wisdom that protected me during my son's slow death.

After a few days, we met with our favorite nurse, Cindy, who was taking care of us and with Liam's neonatologist to take Liam off life-supporting drugs, and oxygen, and monitoring machines. Huddled around Liam's bed, Chris and I held his hands as the neonatologist went through a checklist of heroic measures that we had to decide to request for Liam or not. Tears streamed down our faces. Tears welled in their eyes too.

Defibrillation? No.

Drugs? No, except for anti-seizure medication.

Oxygen Machine? No.

Blow-by Resuscitation? No.

Nasogastric Nutritional Support? My breath caught in my throat, my heart skipped. "What? What are you saying? I don't understand what you're asking. I don't know what to do." Chris understood fully but couldn't make that decision yet either. He took my hand in his. Our nurse calmed me with a soft touch on my shoulder, and a steady gaze, "it's okay, you don't have to decide this now. It probably won't come to that," she said.

When we left the hospital to bring Liam home on hospice care, the doctors said that if they had to estimate how much time Liam had to live they would say a week, or maybe two at the most. It was possible he could live longer, but not probable.

Who can say anything for sure?

The Surprising Comfort
of Snowflakes

I held so many people in my suitcase heart
that I had to let the whole thing go
It was taken by the wind and snow and
still I didn't know that I was waiting . . .
—*The Weepies*

A RRIVING IN FRANKFURT, we chose the Manhattan Hotel from an information board at the airport; it seemed like it would be an easy walk from the station once we took the train into town. If the first thing a person noticed about India was its ancientness, the first thing I noted about Frankfurt was its cleanliness. For some reason, it was an overwhelming relief to be in such a clean place. My mind was so cluttered with the struggle to find clarity on the recent past that to be in a surrounding that had some order and reason lifted a weight from me that I didn't know I was carrying. In Germany even the public trash system was ordered, with clear directions to follow. On almost every corner there was a bin for trash and a bin for recycling.

When we checked into the hotel it was early in the morning. As we got off the elevator we started down the darkened hallway, and after a few steps our passage was suddenly illuminated. The lights were on motion sensors to save energy. Chris was impressed that even the hotels were environmentally minded. I just found it comforting to know that for a while I could count on my dark path being lighted without any effort from me. After traveling through so much darkness and disorder, a thing as simple as a well-lit hall was a relief.

Our room was modern and austere in its design. The beds were black lacquer platforms with plush mattresses and fluffy down comforters. The bathroom had a huge tub and, almost immediately, I sank into it up to my nose. I floated in the hot water and thought of Liam in my womb; I wished that I could have him there again where he was safe, before the beginning of his long dying that started the minute he was cut free from the maternal ocean of his amniotic sac.

When I was able to drag myself from the bath, I was still feeling pretty sick with the bug I'd caught from our sojourn in the East. I only had energy to crawl under the sheets and wrap myself in down—sightseeing would have to wait. Chris didn't seem too disappointed. He was pretty tired too. I was completely drained, and I slept for most of the day and the early evening.

I FELT A BIT BETTER after sleeping, so we walked several blocks to a main square to find something to eat. We treated ourselves to a nice dinner at a restaurant called Oscar's with candles, stemware, and dark mahogany woodwork. A really nice meal is the one indulgence on which Chris will happily spare no expense. Chris ordered wine and a couple of courses. I ordered less since it was the first time in almost a week that I was able to eat anything at all. I remember a pasta dish with a soothing cream sauce. We splurged and ordered a dessert. It felt good to be sharing something sweet again, and be enveloped in pale candlelight, and each other's company. Though we had been together almost constantly for the last five months, there were times when I think both of us felt like the only company we had been keeping was our own demons.

In the main marketplace the next day we strolled through the shopping plaza. The window displays were ready for the Western holidays. It was cold. I was layered in all the warmer clothes that I brought in my pack topped with a Gore-Tex jacket. We hadn't expected to be in Europe till later in the year, so I wasn't really prepared for the weather. In Germany, I found the cold a surprising comfort. I was a wound that needed to be soaked clean, and dressed in a cold pack, and coaxed to healing with comfort and sweetness and splendor.

The air smelled crisp. We passed bakeries. The smell of bread and strudels filled me with warmth. I didn't stick out so much in the streets as an obvious tourist, so the anonymity and lack of unwanted attention from the locals was a relief. I felt like nothing and I wanted to be left alone to walk through the streets unnoticed like a ghost. Liam's sick body was always so cold and I worried that he suffered, though he showed no signs that he did. When he slipped away, his body becoming colder still, snow-cold, maybe that was a comfort to him . . .

The shop windows were lavishly displayed. There were nativities and cherubs all around. I don't believe in one heaven, but sometimes in India it made me sad to think that Liam could be reborn into a state of poverty like much of what I'd seen. I wanted him to be someplace full of splendor where I would one day see him again. I wasn't yet sure how to reconcile what I wanted to believe with the path that chose to speak to my heart, but crossing back to the Western world I chose not to forsake the Dharma just because I didn't understand it all. I don't believe in one all-powerful creator, but I believe in compassion and divinity. I don't believe in one messiah, but I do believe in the power of even the smallest infant to change the world. I believe that a human birth is an almighty precious karmic event, but I don't believe in preserving a life at all costs. I had left the land of the Dharma where the path began, but the Dharma was still in me and I was still on the path.

The festive and bright decorations of Christmas were cheerful, but a sad reminder; a good part of the world was celebrating a miraculous baby boy, one singular birth. I was missing my own guiding star as I stumbled ahead on my long mourning walk around the world, speculating in rebirth. And I was finding comfort in the fact that I was still able to relish joy, and cheer, and laughter; my own at times and other's if that's all I could. I carried a manageable pack on my back, but at home in storage was a heavy, old, square leather suitcase packed before we left with Liam's more precious and personal things: his first ultrasound, cards, a small purple bear wearing one of his tiny diapers, syringes, *Horton Hears a Who!*, empty prescription bottles, *The Runaway Bunny*, a tiny stethoscope, a cotton cap with colorful circus animals, and a death certificate.

The lighted carousels of the winter markets twirled slowly around with smiling children riding ponies, and I rode my thoughts home to my suitcase heart.

That evening we had an early dinner at a quaint restaurant called Das Wirtshaus. As we were ending our meal with warm apple strudel, a light snow began to fall. The flakes closest to the window glowed golden with the light flooding out from the restaurant. In the distance across the square the flakes stood out, specks of white, against the velvet night. A cold snowstorm was building. I began to comprehend how wisdom plays through perception; the falling snow had every potential of getting ugly and uncomfortable, but undeniably, I could see beauty there too by holding a snowflake, each one born so different, small, delicate, complex, unique, fragile—and melting away before my eyes.

Walking through the almost deserted cobblestone square, the tiny flakes touched us and dissolved. Through the falling snow I saw a woman in the distance standing next to an ornate fountain. She was lit from behind by a streetlight, and all I could see was her silhouette. Her voice was ethereal, the most sublime voice I'd ever heard in my life. She sang an aria in German. Her body was encased in darkness, but the voice coming from it was so light, and clear, and enchanting. I was happily astonished that something so lovely, radiating such splendor, and strength, and compassion could come from such a dark, shadowed place.

Memories Like Poppies and Ammunition

Do we see
the world whole
or do we understand
it's wholeness in
it's fragments?
—*Squeak Carnwath*

OUR PLANE RESERVATIONS had us scheduled to leave from Frankfurt to Vienna in a few days. We decided to make a side trip by train to Belgium, to the city of Brugge.

Part of Brugge's allure is its history. Some of the castles and buildings date back to the medieval age. It is one of the few towns to be spared from the destruction of World War I. The nearby towns and fields held the blood of thousands of young men, some not really more than boys. The countryside absorbed the tears, and fears, and frustrations, and rage, of widows and suddenly childless mothers. But still in the heart of all that sadness was a place of comfort, a picturesque town of castles and canals surrounded by walls and moats. When we arrived in the evening the rain was falling hard and cold. Though we didn't think the 't Geerwijn Bed and Breakfast was far from the train station, we got a taxi to spare ourselves from the downpour. It was a quaint building with a pointed brick façade that was typical of the houses in that part of the country. We checked in and spent the night in a warm bed listening to the rain fall all around us.

The next few days were spent wandering around the town square under the massive belfry. I bought chocolates and Chris indulged, as did I, in the rich doupple and tripel bock beers for which Belgium is famous. The season was beginning to turn. The trees lining the canals reflected on the still, narrow waterways. The green was leaving their leaves but their passing, as the foliage began to die, was no less beautiful than the tree in full bloom. At one canal I stopped to look at the town sitting on the motionless canal. The trees had all gone bare. The line between the real trees and buildings and their reflection was nearly imperceptible. The differences between you and me, us and them, life and death, nature and humans, enemy and friend, are as much an illusion as the trees reflected on the surface of the canal. One raindrop on the surface of the canal and the whole image will change, ripples circling outward into one another.

SEVERAL TIMES during our stay in Brugge it was raining too hard for us to go out and walk around. We stayed in the B&B, read, and ate from my stash of chocolate. I read *To Kill a Mockingbird*, which I had picked up in the New Delhi airport. I felt a certain empathy for Jem and his sister. In a similar way that they feared Boo Radley, who lived in the house down the street from them, because he was unknown and hidden, I had feared the unknown moment of death that was hidden in my own home. But when death came, it was gentle and simple, like Boo.

On dryer days we passed time in museums, on tours, and in the local restaurants and shops, indulging in the delicacies of waffles, fries with mayonnaise, chocolate, and beer. We visited an art museum that was housed in one of the city's castles. In it, a huge gothic chapel had been incorporated into the exhibit, suggesting to me that worship and art could be looked at in the same way. The sand-colored stone walls were intricately carved and hollowed out into recessed coves for prayer. The sculptures and artisans left a chiseled testimonial that even in hard places there could be made a space for looking beyond this worldly realm for a better place, for inspiration, and for answers. The paintings were dark, ornate, and complex like lives. Triptychs and diptychs were the convention, as if to convey that any situation or scene was far too full to be communicated in one frame, or along one narrative line. The past and present of any event are hinged and flexible. Past lives are like many framed paintings; our many lives are hinged together. Birth and death are the frames that separate the canvases of lives.

WE WENT ON A DAY-LONG TOUR of the battlefields of the Great War, known as the Fields of Flanders. Our guide, Lode, was born in the nearby town of Passchendaele, which was one of our stops. In Passchendaele we stood in the damp cold air and listened as Lode told us of the four-year-long battle that played out on the field in front of us. Hundreds of men died fighting over a few miles of land. Over the duration of the war hundreds of thousands of lives were lost. The land and the weather itself was just as awesome an enemy as the attacking German army.

In the rainy seasons more men died from drowning in the muddy trenches where they ate, and slept, and fought than were killed by gunfire. A labyrinthine path of wooden planks was set up for the field service to cart away the wounded and dead. To fall off the planking could mean death for the aid workers too; they could drown next to the wounded they went to rescue. So much suffering over such little space seemed unfathomable to me. Lode told of these events with passion and detailed rendering.

This was not history to him but family lore passed down. His grandmother lived in Ypres, the town where young soldiers left for the front lines. While her husband was fighting the war, she fled that town with her fourteen children and one wheelbarrow. For a woman to make such a desperate move, you could imagine, Lode explained, how bad the suffering was, not only for the soldiers, but for the locals too. The farmers of the area still dig up bullets and unexploded bombs in the poppy-dotted fields. They were the only flowers that would grow in those battlefields during the war because they thrived on the abundant disturbed soil. Since then, poppies have become a symbol of remembrance for that war. Before that, even, in Greco-Roman myths poppies were offerings for the dead. On Remembrance Day people wear red poppies as a sign of recognition for soldiers who have been lost. Perhaps blue poppies are a fitting symbol to remember our sons and daughters who have passed on before us? A sign that our lives have been disrupted by devastation but we'll remember to try to stay open to life's abundant blessings, an honorary offering for our daughters and sons, as we battle through the blue days ahead. As we drove down the narrow roads between the fields, Lode pointed out live shells resting against electrical poles. There is a company that scours the back roads looking for live ammunition to pick up and bring to a repository.

To me those bombs seemed like the seeds of our karma. An action can explode immediately or it can be buried in the fields of our future, and even then it might not detonate. It might just be transferred to the repository of an even more distant future. Bombs were nestled in my poppy mind-field. We wandered through abandoned trenches and an Australian dugout that had been recently discovered, complete with bunk beds. We walked among the peaceful graves on fields that rumbled with battle for years. We walked through craters on the preserved and infamous Hill 60, nicknamed "Hell with the lid off" because of the savage battles to control the coveted view. Some of the craters were large enough to be seen from the air.

At times during the tour I was moved to tears by Lode's stories. I felt dwarfed by the open fields and sky, and felt Lilliputian when Lode recreated before my eyes the lives and deaths that were played out on the ground beneath my feet. I was at the same time assuaged and distraught by the realization that life does go on despite disproportional suffering, irreplaceable losses, and life-altering battles.

ONE EVENING we went to dinner in the marketplace that was only a two-minute walk from our B&B. We were probably halfway through our meal when I noticed a long table in the center of the room. At one end was a couple with an infant. At the other end there were six disabled adults with a chaperone. I was stunned by the juxtaposition of the two parties seated at the same table. To anyone else it might not have seemed so ironic, but to me it looked like the extreme possible outcomes of my pre-journey life had been set out in the pans of a scale.

Hinged together at that table were two inaccessible at-one-time futures of some alternate existence, neither of which were my story anymore. Our narrative—like life's important and formative moments—swirls as do eddies in a tidal pool, washing in and out with the ocean. They are flashes of insight, incidental jewels strung together like dewdrop-pearls on a web, or lives linked in a matrix of reincarnation—a trip around the world, one country to another, this life to the next—each one discreet, but reflective of each other in its luster and held together by a common thread, that thread of nothingness that weaves together all beings.

Our lives are not one distinct entity entering another consecutively. It's like blowing the ethereal seed-orb of a flower into the wind. The one shape held loosely together by the finest filaments quietly explodes, pieces of its potential selves falling here and there as determined by the actions of life, and the force that loosed it from its downy blossom carries the seeds on to many unexploded futures.

I believe that Liam can be a newborn in another mother's arms, and also here embracing the back of my neck looking over my shoulder when we need each other. I trust I can meet him in a beautiful and able form I recognize in this life. And I will meet him again as strangers in many other lives. We will all come to that moment. We will breathe, and then we will not. We will be here now and nowhere and everywhere.

WHEN WE WERE PACKING to leave Brugge, I discovered that my bag of exposed film was missing. I had shot over seventy-five rolls of film.

"How could you lose them, Chris?" I was furious. "You know how important those pictures are to me."

"Well, why didn't you carry them, then?" he snapped.

"I didn't have any room in my pack. I guess I should have made room since you don't care about my feelings." I was devastated.

"How do you know I lost them?"

"You had them last." I was speaking about the rolls of film, but unintentionally I had given him the unreasonable responsibility of carrying my feelings too; they were more than I could bear.

As we walked to the train station in a swell of light flurries, we fought the whole way. On the platform, waiting for the train, I noticed for the first time how dangerously close I always stood to the tracks and the oncoming trains as if I were poised for a decision. When we took our seats we discussed seriously the option of not staying together. I wasn't certain that we would find peace with either our loss or each other.

In Belgium I had begun to take things in again: dark chocolate, ornate and gilded art, strong beer, history's story of bloody battles at the Fields of Flanders cratered in my mind with my own bunkered-down battle, savory fresh pommes frites, un-possible outcomes, classic stories of overcoming fear and making connections.

Buried in our future is our past, as vital as poppies and unexploded ammunition.

Awake to a Sudden Fluttering
of Life All Around

But I don't believe in ends. Times past are not times gone as
long as they live inside you . . . I'm the past and I'm the now
and, in rare moments, I believe I've the future in me too.
—*Thomas Moran*

W HEN WE HAD CHECKED OUT OF THE HOTEL in
Frankfurt, to go to Belgium, we forgot to return the key.
That turned out to be a stroke of luck for us, because we
wouldn't have gone back to the hotel if we hadn't. Since we were
there, I insisted that we ask to go to the room again to look for the
missing film. Chris thought I was nuts and that there'd be no hope
of finding it, but he indulged my whim and even said he wanted to
go up to the room and look for it himself.

I sprang toward him with happiness when he got off the elevator holding the bag of film. Chris was excited too, not so much
about the film, but because I wasn't angry anymore and he was off
the hook. It's amazing how quickly emotions and thoughts can turn

around. I realized it was true that the mind is like the sky; sometimes it's covered with clouds and darkness, and just as quickly as
it became obscured it can clear and be bright again. I was learning
that marriage was a bit like that too. Together we were learning to
weather the unexpected storms and enjoy the bright days.

We had an evening to explore before our flight left for Vienna in
the morning. We stayed at the vintage Victoria Hotel. We strolled the
tree-lined streets of the Sachsenhausen section of the town, which is
the older, more prestigious section. We wandered in one of Europe's
most well-known Christmas markets just a block off the Main River.
In the market the square was lit by hundreds of strung bulbs and
carousel lights. The night around us was filled with a honey-yellow
glow. Again, I was struck by the sad beauty of the carousel. The
ponies went up and down like emotions, and the gilded parade went
round and round like life after life on the karmic, samsaric wheel.

Every day, every fight, every kind gesture could be a beginning,
or an end. Or both.

VIENNA WAS ELEGANT with gilded coffee and opera houses. The
holiday ball season would be starting soon, and while we wouldn't
be in India celebrating Buddhist-style, I began to anticipate the holiday and the prospect of attending a traditional Viennese Ball with
chamber music and dancing. Since we thought we'd stay a while,
we booked accommodations for an efficiency apartment rather than
booking a hotel. The first day we did a bit of shopping to stock the
small fridge and settled into the little suite.

I, rightly or not, judge a town by its bookstores, newspapers,
and coffee shops. I think, maybe, these things let me in on how
much the people around value communication.

I particularly like the bookstore Shakespeare and Co. in Paris—
an outpost for the expatriates of the '20s, and still a refuge for way-

farers, writers, and wanderers to the Left Bank today. I knew that there was a sister store in Vienna, so we set out on a little mission to find it. It was a good excuse to get us out and about in town to see what we would find. At the bookstore, I decided on *When Nietzsche Wept* by Irvin Yalom, since Nietzsche was one of Vienna's most well-known residents. Plus, I was struck by the similarities between Buddhism and existentialism.

Over the next few days I devoured the book. In stately coffee houses, drinking café Viennese served in small cups on silver trays, I also perused the many daily papers hung on wooden dowels.

The icy rain continued to fall all during our stay; we were continually turned in to the cafés by the weather, and my mind was turned inward, too. I don't remember a lot of the sights and sounds of Vienna as well as I remember what I read there. *When Nietzsche Wept* turned out to be a light-switch for me. That work of fiction sparked insight that illuminated my reality with its imagined therapeutic relationship between Freud, Nietzsche, and Josef Breuer, one of the founding fathers of psychoanalysis.

Yalom writes that growth is not the only reward of pain, that creativity and discovery are begotten there too. He quotes Nietzsche: "One must have chaos and frenzy within oneself to give birth to a dancing star." I felt for sure that I had given birth to a dancing star when Liam passed from this life, but now that that star was beyond my reach, the chaos and frenzy seemed to consume me. Yalom writes in Nietzsche's voice: "Because death comes—that does not mean that life has no value."

If I were given the choice to relive the last few months since Liam's birth exactly as they were, or not to have him at all, without hesitation, I would choose to give birth to Liam and the dancing star he became for me. In that pain, I discovered what a meaningful life means to me.

It is said of a midwife in Yalom's book that she found a passion for life in the moment after a child was born and before it took its first breath because she was "renewed . . . by immersion in that moment of mystery, that moment that straddles existence and oblivion." I had been immersed in that mysterious moment between oblivion twice—before Liam's first breath and just after his last. I needed to find a way to create some meaning out of those mysteriously gifted moments that would renew my optimism; proof that I was suffering not because I was being punished, but because suffering will lead to some good discovery beyond my current ability to fathom it.

It seemed important to tell my story not because it is unique or more profound than the story of anyone else's loss, but because loss itself is so universal, so basic. There is no one walking through this world who doesn't know, who will not know, death. None of us have the mustard seed that the Buddha sent Kisa Gotami to find. And yet, if we have faith the size of a mustard seed that joy will be victorious, then we might be able to accept that hopefully sorrow can't exist without happiness in the same proportion.

We all suffer. We all want to find a path out of suffering. I chose to leave my life as I knew it and walk a literal path around the world. I hoped that along the way I'd find the right view, stumble on the right thoughts, do the right things, and find the right words to guide me.

CHECKING OUR EMAIL one day in Vienna, Chris and I were surprised to hear from our friend who was caretaking our house that there was a big problem with the tenant that he wasn't able to handle. Once again we found that our plans were unexpectedly changing. The renter had sent a letter to our friend saying that he had done some research into the rental market, and decided that the price we agreed on for rent was too expensive. So, he calculated that he had already paid enough to cover the next three months and therefore he wouldn't be paying any more rent. He also concluded that we had no choice but to accept his actions because it would take at least three months for us to evict him, and by then the lease would be up. He signed off saying that he hoped we were recovering from the recent death of our son and that we shouldn't take his decision personally because it was only business.

Needless to say, we were astounded by his ignorance and audacity. Our trip had come to an abrupt end with that letter. We had no interest in arguing with him over the matter, and we didn't have enough money to continue to travel and pay the mortgage on our house since the rent he paid only covered ninety percent as it was. We found the nearest phone after getting our friend's email and called him to get all the details.

Chris then called our renter and told him that we were surprised that he was so unhappy with his living situation and that it wasn't our intention to exploit anyone. We had priced the rent fairly, and if he disagreed then we'd be happy to take his letter as a thirty-day notice. Chris told the renter that we'd be home in thirty days, and we expected him to agree to be gone. Otherwise we'd be home in two days to deal with the matter in person. I think he was surprised that we responded so quickly to his letter, and saw that he'd be in for a fight if he tried to carry out his plan, so he agreed to move out in a month. I was furious, but also not surprised: most of the plans we had made in the recent past seemed to lead us down a completely different path than we had expected.

The day before we were scheduled to leave, we spent most of the day at a butterfly conservatory called the Schmetterlinghaus. The air inside was humid and warm and it was tropical compared to the cold rain outside. The butterfly house was in the Burggarten, a park in the center of town that was transformed from the private estate of a baron. The greenhouse housing thousands of species of tropical butterflies was built onto the back wall of the old city. There was something reassuring in that juxtaposition of a brick wall and an unexpected tropical oasis.

The first time we took Liam outside the walls of the NICU, Chris and I took him for a walk around the children's garden at Emmanuel Hospital. We sat with him under a tree and enjoyed the sun on our skin for the first time in days. We hadn't left the hospital except when the nurses changed shifts and we were required to leave the ward. For Liam it was the very first time he felt the sun. In the hospital's garden there was a brick path that swirled around the small plot of land, which was enclosed on all sides by the hospital walls. There were colorful plants, herbs, and cheerful sculptures of turtles and other creatures. The bricks were engraved with the names and dates of the children who had passed before us.

In the hospital's enclosed garden, there was also a plaque on the wall in a section planted with flowers to attract the butterflies. It was a quote by Mark Twain: "What the caterpillar knows to be the end, the butterfly knows to be the beginning." Liam's brain damage had encased him in a cocoon, unable to reach out to anyone around him. And yet, I believed that I could see a spark of awareness in his eyes at times. I believed that some of his gesticulations were intended and not just a product of muscle seizures. It may have been my wishful thinking. To become more, to embody his karmic potential, he needed to go beyond the cocoon of his body.

In Vienna, we spent most of the afternoon walking around the small tropical greenhouse, beside miniature waterfalls, and sometimes right through trees where the trunks had been carved out to make way for the path. It was easy to miss all the life that was fluttering around, but when I stood still and paid attention, the whole room seemed to come suddenly alive, teeming with silent fluttering wings. It was like an optical illusion: when you stare at something long enough and another image appears. Only in this house of butterflies, it wasn't a stagnant image that suddenly appeared, but movement and life replacing stillness and confinement.

It was hard not to think of Liam in that place. The blue of a butterfly's wing was like his eyes. The amber spots on another reminded me of his hair. The red of another resting on a flower reminded me of his tiny mouth.

That temperate butterfly house alive with silent beings unbound and fluttering around me was an unexpected and pleasant surprise in the middle of a bitter winter.

We were nearing the end of our trip, but it was also a beginning.

Turning Wheels

Accustomed, as I've been, to contemplating both nirvana
and samsara as inherent in myself, I had forgotten
to think of hope and fear.
—*Milarepa*

ETTING OFF A TRAIN IN PRAGUE'S STATION I saw a
woman walking quickly toward us. Before I could look away,
I thought I saw a panicked look in her eyes. I thought she
needed help—maybe her kid was lost somewhere in the station, I
thought. Opening my gaze to hers, I let her approach.

"You need room?" she said pointing to the map that had several
circles drawn on it. "I have good room. Clean, good price." She
pointed to one of the circles around Staromestska radnice, "Oldest
square in Praha. No stay, just look."

"Just look?" I asked thumbing my shoulder straps and hopping
a little to help hoist my pack to tug the straps down tighter. I ques-
tioned Chris with my eyes.

"I have a metro ticket for you," she tried to entice us, "I will take
you there. If you don't like it you no stay and still I pay for the
metro."

Chris repeated the terms to make sure we had understood. "If we don't like it, we don't have to pay?"

"*Ne,*" she nodded firmly.

"And you pay for the metro?" I added.

"*Ano,*" again a firm nod.

"No?" I asked, glancing at Chris.

Her hands shot up in front of her, palms toward me. I'd misunderstood somehow. "Sorry, yes, yes," she pumped the air for emphasis. I later learned that *ano* means "yes" in Czech. Chris and I agreed with a what-have-we-got-to-lose shrug of our shoulders.

The voice of the conductor had the cadence of a Bohemian folk dancer. The metro wasn't crowded. There were no other travelers like us that I could see. December must have been a slow month for tourism in Prague. Our guide was silent, patting the air in front of her hip at each stop—not yet, not yet. Czechs boarded and deboarded, lips straight as pencils, shoulders hung low. The conducting voice sang out the name of the stops. I recalled the word *Staromestska* from the map. Our guide sprung through the sliding doors and motioned for us to follow, darting between pillars and people. We followed her lead to the escalator.

It was the steepest escalator I'd ever seen. I was forced to lift my chin up higher than I'd been able to muster for the last three months. The escalator felt nearly vertical as we rode up for the first time. In a row on both the walls all the way up the narrow passage were dozens of frames meant to hold advertisements, but, oddly enough and seemingly auspicious to me, they each held the same picture of the Buddha: long lobes, stylized curls and blue bindi knot, gaze and lips resting in an expression of natural great peace. I was comforted to unexpectedly find him. Ascending, I passed through an honor-guard of sacred symbols. I wasn't following the itinerary I thought I needed to, but I was on the right path. We rose to the surface while the golden glow of Kaprova Street's lights enveloped us into the amber Prague night.

Parizska street and Dlouha street were laid at just the right angles so that as we walked west, Saint Nicholas Church on the left and the Old Town Hall on the right seemed to simultaneously step aside, extending like arms to hold open invisible gates as we entered Old Town Square, Staromestske nam. Tyn Church with her twin Romanesque towers, topped with black peaks that were punctuated with golden stars, reigned over the square. The fine dusting of snow glittered on top making it look more magical. The town looked like a fairy tale. I desperately needed a happy ending. Since, like most fairy tales, my tale also began with peril and misfortune.

Our escort from the station brought my gaze back to reality with a heavy swipe of her hand through my line of vision, "Come, come. Not far." She pointed to the cobblestone Tynska street, which was more of a passageway, really. She led us across the square. We slipped down Tynska. Again, streets laid at odds begged buildings that had stood for hundreds of centuries to step aside, revealing the continuing path; I walked toward what looked like a dead end and suddenly there was a way out, a path I didn't see around a building's corner. We walked on to Number 12—our for-the-meantime home. I wouldn't be staying long, but I knew right away that tucked-away apartment in that snowy, shimmering town was the right place for now.

I was handed the skeleton key to the outer door and had to push hard to open the wooden Baroque door in opposition to the iron hinges that held on tight.

Number 12 Tynska was a small studio apartment: one full bed, a table, wardrobe, sparkling clean bathroom with washer and dryer, in the corner an efficiency kitchen. I felt safe there, like I could really rest for the first time in months.

When I turned on the TV, the screen sparked into focus. "Oh, honey. Look, it's Tootsie," I said. That movie was a joke Chris and I shared. At home, when I told Chris that I was sick and needed to watch *Tootsie* and drink Theraflu, he knew that I was really, really sick. One New Year's Eve, when we were too sick to go out, we had rented that movie and for a time we forgot for a little bit how bad we felt. I always joked that a person couldn't help feeling better after a sappy movie like that.

"Do you feel better already?" Chris asked.

Not understanding the Czech dubbing, I didn't watch for long and switched to CNN. Fundamentalists in Iraq were angry and vowing revenge for the bombings. A billionaire in a high-tech hot air balloon raced to be the first person to circle the globe. He glided above the polluted seas, starving children, warring nations, and rerouted around China, whose officials denied him permission to float through the air above them.

IN THE HOLIDAY MARKET in the square, shoppers gathered around great tin tubs of fresh fish. They pointed and the vendor, with hands that looked as tough as his leather apron, grabbed the desired one, clutching down just behind its gills that pumped, staccato. The vendor clubbed it, gutted it, weighed it, and wrapped it in the day's old news. Fish was the traditional holiday dinner for Czechs.

Children rode ponies around a ring—a living carousel. The children were swaddled in woolen coats, mittens, scarves, and hats, the same bright colors of the large umbrella that covered the ring: red, yellow, green, and blue—a cosmic kaleidoscope on a simulated samsaric wheel.

I watched for an hour or so, and imagined Liam going round and round with the other children, happy.

. . .

ON THE OTHER SIDE of the square in the Old Town Hall I went, one day, to see an exhibit of photos—Czech Press Photos.

Standing in front of the photos I was so captivated I felt the sad pain and tearful joy of all the people looking back at me from their stilled moments. I imagined the bulbs flashing.

Flash: Czechs overflowed the streets smiling and holding flags. The women's hockey team had just won the Gold Medal.

Flash: on a catwalk surrounded by blank-faced spectators a naked woman knelt in front of a man with her mouth open guiding him to her with her hand at a Sex Industry Trade Show.

Flash: wedding, smiles, flowers in midair.

Flash: Clinton met Havel, the President/writer of the Czech Republic, blue shirt, red ties, extended hands, straight spines, and lines of dignitaries with frozen smiles.

Flash: yachters raced for the cup, sails full.

Flash: a World Cup match, a muddy, muscular player suspended in midair, toes pointed down like a dancer, hair splashing up around the ball he had just head-butted.

Flash: the woman held up a picture of herself taken before the man hunted her down in the streets of Bangladesh and doused her with battery acid that ate her flesh to the bone. In the picture that she held, her mouth was as straight as her long black hair. Her dark eyes were wide. Could she see the future? In the larger photo before me, her hair was still straight but her face was a swirling eddy of scar tissue and reconstructed flesh. Her mouth was half devoured by a bottle of acid in the hand of a man who tried to take her life, and knew he'd at least take her prospects of marriage, because he wouldn't take no for an answer. And yet, she smiled for the more recent photo and her eyes were brighter than before. Could she see a different future? Had that searing suffering transformed something else in her life?

Flash: the baby's skin was vellum. Ribs protruded, belly and cheeks sagged sallow, and eyes were set deep, cast in the shadow of his skull. Why was that baby dying? Did he know his mother loved him? Closing my eyes, the darkness only developed the image further. Liam was so thin in the days just before his death. His bones were hard against my hands even through his clothes and blankets. His eyes too were sunken and dark. When his ashes were returned to me in a tiny box wrapped with blue paper I wasn't surprised by how small the box was but by how little it weighed. It was not heavier than the images that were hanging before me. It was not heavier than the album of photos of Liam, those photos I composed to be my artful memories. Photos like the beautiful still-lifes of the Dutch masters who called them *le mort naturel*—the natural death. Still-lifes that say as much about what is not in the frame as about what is there. In the end Liam was not heavier than a thick book, maybe barely heavier than this one.

Flash: my pictures.

Flash: your pictures.

Flash: same exposures; same burn and dodge; same fix; still life, mort naturel; a life stilled, and yet still a life.

IN PRAGUE'S OLD TOWN SQUARE, there were songs and light and snowfall one night. Flakes fluttered toward my cup of mulled wine, disappearing as they met the rising steam to make nothing.

People gathered around two men who were playing guitars. They were singing, in Czech, an American rock song about knockin' on doors. People wore warm smiles and passed a flask to protect them from the cold, huddling close and not minding the snow a bit. Their voices rose to the top of the streetlight, to the bright star on top of the shimmering hundred-foot balsam fir dressed for the holiday before the closed doors of Tyn Church, and up to the hands of the enormous medieval astrological clock, or *Orloj*, at the top of the tower on the opposite side of the square. Crafted and cast in 1410 it has been plotting, faithfully and gracefully, the ecliptic—the sun's apparent path during the year—and the state of the universe with its rotating earth and sky dials, zodiac rings, and orbiting sun and moon icons for the people gathered below looking up. The song of the crowd and my eyes rose up further still and I was lifted too, just high enough to see a time in the distance when I could think of Liam, or see his picture, and smile instead of cry. We all waited for the stroke that would set the wheels on the Orloj in motion. The great gold gears would turn; the bells peal; figurines of the faithful and some representing vanity, greed, and hatred, and a statue of the Grim Reaper ringing a knell and turning an hourglass upside-down, would parade out through open windows from the darkness inside the tower to dance around the moon and stars on the clock's face.

Late in the night, maybe it might have been the hour turning into a new day, Czechs and foreigners, babies in strollers, old men and women, lovers, nuns in habits, all of us travelers on a compulsory journey, gathered in the square beneath the ornate Orloj. Sparklers and candles were handed throughout the crowd. Light was passed wick to wick, person to person. Each life we live is like the flame from one candle passed to another. It's not the same flame, but it's not entirely different either. I was on the verge of starting over. I wasn't entirely different, but I wasn't the same. Sparklers sputtered flecks of light like departing souls, and flames bowed to the Czech symphony performing on the stage in the snow-dusted square. There was song.

Though it was not in my language, I felt it was about hope and happiness.

Beyond, Beyond

Yes, as everyone knows, meditation and water
are wedded for ever.
—*Herman Melville*

I STILL HAD A LOT OF WATER TO TREAD before I could be
at peace. Once we arrived home, each holiday or special
anniversary, as hard as they were, seemed like I was moving a
bit further. I looked for a meaningful occupation, still searching for a
reason, and a way to revise my future.

But I had learned from diving that being underwater could be
disorienting. You may think you're swimming up when really you
are swimming down. For the next year or so I thought I was coming to the surface of my grief, until one day I realized I had been
moving the wrong direction.

I WASN'T AWARE that not getting through it—falling apart, shat-
tering completely—was actually an option, though I had days and
weeks that seemed like my blackening mind-spiral would go on for-

ever. I had nights—nights when other new parents would have been rocking their crying child to sleep—that I was in bed sobbing so hard Chris couldn't even understand me. Once in my thrashing misery I threw myself off the bed and beat myself against the floor. I could not get my body physically low enough to meet my heart and mind. If the ground opened and swallowed me it would not have been low enough.

I had moments when my howling cries startled even me. The sounds were so raw they seemed to be coming from all directions at me instead of from the darkness in me. Maybe I sensed nothing would be fixed if I let go that way, if I made more than a scratch with the knife on my wrist even though I bore down with the sharp edge till veins popped blue. I could not slice. And when Chris saw my wrists later he held me calmly and spoke close to my face, "Promise me you won't leave." I think I said okay but I still drove way too fast in the dark on wet and twisting Terwilliger Boulevard coming home at the ends of the days.

There had been those times in our trip around the world that I found myself too close to the tracks, keeping my secret that I would have just as soon thrown myself under most of those trains that I instead got on and kept moving. Now, several times waiting for the bus once we returned home, I noticed I stood so close to the street that my toes hung over the ledge of the curb.

I thought all the searching for a meaningful occupation was going to reward me with a higher meaning, a reason for hanging on. I thought I'd been swimming up away from the sadness. But I'd been diving down. Suddenly, I was even deeper in than I knew I could go, in the abyssal waters of my despair, treading through pain I was too afraid to thoroughly feel. I was nearly crushed by the pressure that had been building up.

One evening after work as the bus pulled away from the stop

where I was still standing, I thought, "Shit, I missed the bus," and then realized slowly after many fuzzy brooding moments what I really meant, "Shit! I missed my chance to get in front of it."

I was no longer sure I could trust myself.

RELYING SOLELY on the tenacious need to know it all meant something—to prove I'd not lost everything for nothing—was holding me back up till then. When I got home I called a psychologist accepting now I needed a little help to make sense of my journey, all the meaningful sites I'd seen, and the sacred sorrow it left welled up inside me. The receptionist said I could come in an hour. When I got to the doctor's office the psychologist said there had been a mistake and that she wasn't taking new patients, but I could come in and talk to her for a few minutes anyway. I began to speak to her through a torrent of tears. She didn't send me away.

It was time to stop trying to somehow outswim my fear. I let, finally, the leering shark get me, the one just under the surface, waiting to attack the whole time that I thought I was going to feel fine. I finally had to, was glad to, let the fear of desolation go. The water carried me away.

We humans are made up by a good percentage of water; we are little else. Our bodies are formed in water and we're birthed out of that fluid place. We are oceans. We are tears. We are raindrops and puddles. Water is lethal and life-giving—rising tides, breaking waters, sustenance. We are rivers rushing. We are the hot water bathing and steeping sacred leaves that swirl like eddies. Water in a bowl is a simple universal offering; we all have that much to give. Water offers shores and burning ghats from where we can embark, to set out seeking, and to return to our chaotic home ground where, if we're mindful, we can realize wisdom is at play within the unspeakable blessings of life.

I was more than a bit afraid to be there, sitting still with my devastation and observing the tidal waves of emotion in my mind. I unpacked my heart and cried for months and talked my way back to the surface.

I BEGAN TO KNOW that pain like that doesn't go away from you and you can't get away from it; it has to go through you. I put myself on the pyre of desolating guilt and let the buried-in-my-bones misery burn me up. In my mind, I felt like I was dying. I let the pain I feared for so long—stared in the face and beat back for more than a year and a half—devour and swallow me whole. It consumed me.

Far Beyond Beyond

The world of dew,
is the world of dew.
And yet, and yet . . .
—*Issa*

I HAD RESIGNED MYSELF TO CARRYING some amount of sadness forever, and yet I slowly gave myself over to the possibility of bearing a greater share of happiness too.

It would be a long time before I could again trust the world was, for the most part, good. And yet three years after Liam had gone, for the first time, I was not so dulled that I didn't noticed the springtime moving in with its lingering light and its promise of warmth. I wouldn't have believed it, and yet, I now feel I've been opened up further than I thought possible to delight in many unexpected ways. For years I felt tense and even physically ill in the week leading up to Liam's birthday, knowing I'd have to acknowledge that only the numbers of his age were still growing, and I'd have to brace myself for the wash of sadness that would crash down on the anniversary of his death. Every year for those weeks that made up his life, I rededicate myself to mindfulness and trying to generate gratitude.

Every year was a struggle to make the best of it. And yet, on the ninth anniversary of Liam's death, I awoke happy, for a change.

I WAS AT THE MILAREPA BUDDHIST RETREAT CENTER. Even though I was smiling, I was still very blue and mindful all day of Liam's absence. I finally found some time alone in the meditation hall that was a renovated attic of a rustic farmhouse. The sounds of laughing children—two of them, in fact, my own—in the fields below, running under the liquid luminous arch of the water-hose, rose up. Sitting before the altar, cocooned in warmth and the glow of the offering lights, taking in the richly colored thangkas, the tears did come, as they always had. And yet, when I took a breath and let go, as I had many times before, this time the grasping fist of sorrow in me unclenched flat enough so I could hold something else that had been around me too, even while I was experiencing such sadness. I realized my tears were also tears of joy. I was happy to be exactly where I was, knowing every step I took—even the hardest ones that I somehow willed myself to take from a strong place so deep within me that I never knew it existed—was a step I was supposed to take. Unknowingly, I had walked to exactly where I needed to be when I was supposed to be there, even though I thought I was only wandering. A change had come to me, the one that for so long I had held on hoping for . . . For so long, too, I couldn't imagine a world in which I didn't ache to hold my son again. And yet, it finally felt right to hold that ache and embrace joy too; just like I did when Liam was alive. Samsara and nirvana are not two.

THE HURT WAS SO BAD when Liam died it separated me from the world, and yet through the hurt I found my way back, awake with a greater awareness, to the world; "not myself goes home to myself," as the poet Keats said. I believe I did find something on the other side of pain. Even in pieces, I will endure and I know I have it in me to wake up and be happy feeling now for sure these rarely blooming lifetimes are blue poppies on torrents rushing down sacred mountains headed for the ocean of wisdom. When I awoke my son was not with me. I am still in this life rushing by, but not alone without a reason.

Water wedded with meditation carried me to this moment, here. The "me" I am now was birthed from a sorrow-filled voyage. And Tara too, the Mother of Compassion, was born from the Buddha's teardrop. I was never alone on that mourning walk, wandering the world, wondering, journeying further. And yet, and yet . . .

IT WOULD BE A LONG TIME before I would understand the vision I had had at the time Liam died. In that still moment of mystery, I had seen someone, whose face I couldn't then see, pick him up and carry him away. I had thought she might be a protector, a gate-keeper, come to carry him away. I've come to believe that the person walking away who held Liam laughing actually was me, the essence of me. Liam was not calling "Mommy" back over the distance to me moving away. He was actually greeting me, welcoming me to him, when we embraced to go beyond.

I had to die in my mind to wake up to my life. In letting go, samsara *is* nirvana.

Sometimes powerful reasons to hold on are not yet known to us.

Gaté, gaté, paragaté, parasam gaté. Bodhi svaha!

(I am gone, gone; I am going, beyond. Far beyond beyond.
Happiness, Joy Victorious!)

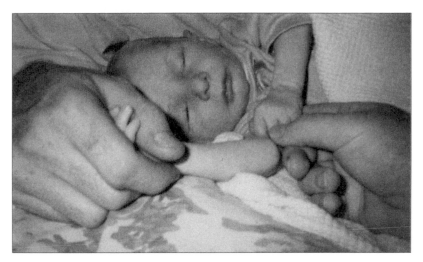

Liam Christopher Morton

For Liam Christopher Morton, because of Liam, to Liam, who saved me from myself and woke me up body, speech, and mind.

For Oliver Hudson Morton (OHM) and Alice Hazel (AH) Morton so they'll really know how much I mean it when I say, "I love you higher than the sun and moon, and deeper than the ocean and sea." And so they'll not have to say they never knew their eldest brother.

For Chris Morton, with gratitude for growing up with me, with love for creating with me our three jewels, with deep affection and abiding friendship as we grow old together.

Acknowledgments

DEEPEST GRATITUDE AND PROFOUND LOVE that reaches far beyond beyond to my greatest guru, Liam Christopher Morton.

With enduring thanks to Oliver, a rough-tumble little buddha-bear of a boy with a heart as wide as his eyes, who sees in the world what others don't—beauty in the ordinary, strength in the ferocious; and Alice, who is everything beautiful, and in all ways able, just beginning to spark with feisty, fierce wisdom and wit, her power is imminent—she's a just-lit firecracker; thanks to both of them for choosing me to be their mother, challenging me, and giving me a reason every day to try to be a better person. Unending thanks, with a full heart, to Chris for creating a life with me to create babies and books—all I've ever wanted to do.

Thanks to my mom, Maureen O'Brien, for always believing I'd

be a published writer, for encouraging me to adventure, take risks, and always do what I felt was right, and being with me when it counts the most—at the bottom. Thanks to Jerry and Philippa Morton for their support.

To His Holiness the Dalai Lama, and Her Eminence Jetsun Chime Luding, and all the Lamas who teach the Dharma, which makes me believe there is joy and meaning beyond the suffering of this life. Thanks to all my sangha members in Portland, Oregon, who were there with us that summer. And to Isabell (Cindy) Soule for telling me Liam's NICU bed was "sacred ground" and creating a supportive space to allow us to make that true. To Sharon Griffin for sitting vigil with us that summer. To Myriam Coppens for being my lifeguard, compassionately and wisely, while I talked to the surface. To the Kurukulla Center in Medford, Massachusetts, and the Milarepa Retreat Center in Vermont, especially Wendy Hobbs, and Ani Tsunma-la (Sue Macy) and Kacia Beznoska for a healing retreat. Special thanks to Kacia for helping me take care of my little joys Oliver and Alice while I ironed the last drafts. Thanks to Acharya Judith Simmer-Brown for her astounding Dakini teachings and for reassuring me I was not mad to think that awful blessings, "gifts of devastation," do exist. With sincere thanks to Wilber Jones, for invoking my success with genuine encouragement assuring me my book would be published after reading my proposal draft, and for all his words of wisdom from then on.

Thanks to Mary Karr, Katherine Harrison, Toi Derricott, Jewell Parker Rhoads, and Michael Ondaatje who unwittingly inspired me with their writing, and whose words at conferences empowered me to take risks. Special thanks to Mary Karr who told an anecdote about defending the content of her writing to her colleague saying, "What else would you have me write about but life, death, and my baby." I took it as permission. Thanks to Chuck

Palahniuk who read the first draft of the first chapter, and said, "This is good, this is important, and we can make it better." And then, he did meet with me to revise. Thanks Annie Callan, in whose workshop on her houseboat I shared the first drafts of subsequent chapters. And thanks to the other writers of that group I call "the moorage writers" for harboring me in my first attempts to articulate my experience.

Thanks to my literary lifeline, the University of New Orleans Low-Residency MFA program, fellow students and professors: without all of you—none of this. Special thanks to Bill Lavender, who said and I believe him, "If you find no beauty in it then there is no point." Many thanks to Dr. Nancy Dixon and Kay Murphy with gratitude and respect and admiration. To my mentor and writing guru, Dinty Moore, for being so generous with his knowledge, humor, and kindness, and for making me believe what I had to say was important, and that I could say it well enough, and for encouraging me to submit the manuscript to Wisdom Publications at the time I did, wrinkles and all.

With enormous gratitude to Josh Bartok at Wisdom Publications who wisely smoothed the wrinkles and brought into existence my little book about Liam's existence and what it all means to me. That he was wearing an "Underdog" T-shirt the day he offered me a contract says it all for me. That this book of Liam will live with Wisdom is a blessing; there could not be a better home.

About the Author

Photo © Mim Atkins

K ATHLEEN WILLIS MORTON holds a MFA in creative writing from the University of New Orleans. She's been practicing Tibetan Buddhism since age 17. She has wanted all her life to be a writer, except in seventh grade when she was encouraged to be practical and she thought about being a lawyer or a dentist. She lives in Cambridge, Massachusetts, with her family, and continues to be impractical every chance she gets. She can be found online at www.TheBluePoppyAndTheMustardSeed.com, and encourages readers to visit and share their experiences on the online forum.

About Wisdom Publications

Wisdom Publications, a nonprofit publisher, is dedicated to making available authentic works relating to Buddhism for the benefit of all. We publish books by ancient and modern masters in all traditions of Buddhism, translations of important texts, and original scholarship. Additionally, we offer books that explore East-West themes unfolding as traditional Buddhism encounters our modern culture in all its aspects. Our titles are published with the appreciation of Buddhism as a living philosophy, and with the special commitment to preserve and transmit important works from Buddhism's many traditions.

To learn more about Wisdom, or to browse books online, visit our website at www.wisdompubs.org.

You may request a copy of our catalog online or by writing to this address:

Wisdom Publications
199 Elm Street
Somerville, Massachusetts 02144 USA
Telephone: 617-776-7416
Fax: 617-776-7841
Email: info@wisdompubs.org
www.wisdompubs.org

The Wisdom Trust

As a nonprofit publisher, Wisdom is dedicated to the publication of Dharma books for the benefit of all sentient beings and dependent upon the kindness and generosity of sponsors in order to do so. If you would like to make a donation to Wisdom, you may do so through our website or our Somerville office. If you would like to help sponsor the publication of a book, please write or email us at the address above.

Thank you.

Wisdom is a nonprofit, charitable 501(c)(3) organization affiliated with the Foundation for the Preservation of the Mahayana Tradition (FPMT).